11-95

11-95

GOOD HOUSEKEEPING
ITALIAN
COOKERY

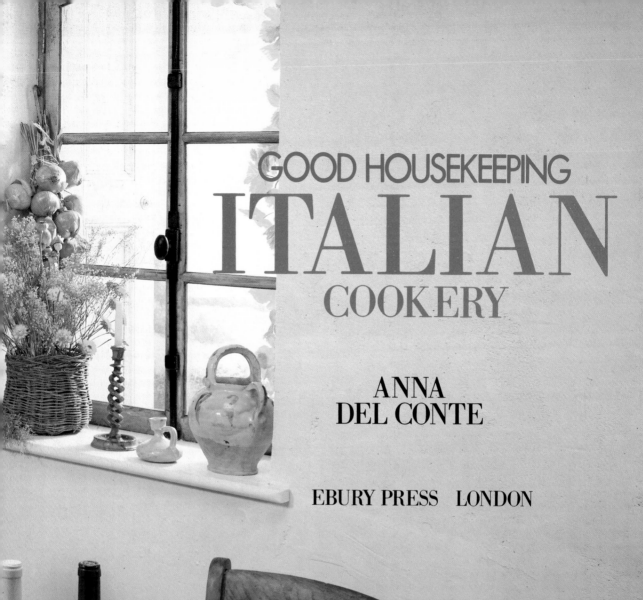

Good Housekeeping
ITALIAN
COOKERY

ANNA
DEL CONTE

EBURY PRESS   LONDON

Published by Ebury Press
National Magazine House
72 Broadwick Street
London W1V 2BP

First Impression 1982

ISBN 0 85223 240 3

'For Oliver'

Design by Design 23
Artist Susanne Lihou
Photography Vernon Morgan
Stylist Maggie Heinz

The Publishers would like to thank the wine producers
Lamberti, Pedrotti & Lungarotti, and their UK agents
Morgan Furze & Gilbey Vintners, for the supply of the
wines featured in the book.

Typeset by Advanced Filmsetters (Glasgow) Ltd
Printed and bound in Yugoslavia by
Mladinska Knjiga, Ljubljana

CONTENTS

Introduction

In the cooking of Italy today the ancient influences of the Greeks and the Etruscans can still be traced. The Etruscan origin is mainly evident in the dishes of central and northern Italy. The cooking of the south is based on Greek tradition, overlaid by the influence of the Arabs.

During the Renaissance the Italian states excelled in cooking as well as in the arts. The banquets of the city states and the various dukedoms were the grandest in Europe. Those of Venice were reputed to be the most magnificent of them all, not only for the food, but also for the elegance of the table, for it was here that the fork and the glass were first introduced. The Italian gastronomic tradition was exported to France by Caterina de' Medici when, in 1533, she married the future King Henri II. Her cooks, and later those of Maria de' Medici, the mother of Louis XIII, not only taught the French their culinary skills, but also brought with them such delicacies as *petits pois*, artichokes, spinach, and 'French' beans—all vegetables now undeservedly associated with French cuisine.

But these sumptuous banquets were not everyday fare; that was, and still is, homely, simple and, most of all, regional. In Italy people do not talk of Italian cooking but rather of the cooking of, say, Bologna, Sicily or Rome, since each region, and even each city or town, has its special culinary accent, just as it has its own particular dialect. This is understandable since the country has only been united for just over a century.

Geographically Italy extends from the Alps, highest mountains in Europe, in the north, more than 950 kilometres (600 miles) to the parched soil of Sicily in the south. The Appenine mountains run all the way down its spine and the terrain, apart from the very fertile Po valley, is mostly rocky and unyielding. This has forced the Italian peasant to cultivate every possible piece of flat land, as you will see if you journey by train or car down the peninsula. Wherever possible, there will be beautiful olive groves, rich vegetable gardens and small vineyards perched high on the mountains and apparently inaccessible.

When in Italy, always ask to be served with 'what the locals eat'. Do not ask for *spaghetti alla marinara* in Milan, or for *risotto con osso buco* in Naples. Just as the food is regional, so is it seasonal. Baked dish are eaten in the winter, as are all the heavy braised cuts of meat. At Easter, the first salad, *soncino* (corn lettuce), appears on the table, opening the season to an immense variety of salads which culminate in the autumn with the most delicious of them all: *radicchio rosso trevisano*, pale purple-red chicory leaves which have a very special taste.

In Italy there is no *haute cuisine*. The best cooking is that done in the home, *cucina casareccia*. Preparing food is not a science, but a creative activity which differs in the hands of each cook. When I ask my Italian friends for the recipe of some wonderful dish they have served me, their instructions are always rough and ready: a handful of this, a pinch of that, a glass of something else (and the glass is never the same size)!

This highly individual home-cooking is emphasised by the importance given by the Italians to the family table, where everyone gathers to enjoy the ritual of eating. Children and teenagers are expected to sit down with their parents to share family life, to relax and talk before going off again to different activities.

An Italian meal is seldom if ever an elaborate affair. A great many of the dishes are cooked at the last minute. When pasta is eaten, for example, the family is called to table the moment the pasta is put into the saucepan, so that everybody is sitting down by the time it is ready. Fried food, a method of cooking of which the Italians are masters, should be eaten as soon as it is ready. The cook stands at the stove, frying, and passes over delicious morsels of *frittelle*, *ravioli*, tiny bunches or slices of vegetables, courgette flowers, apples and even cubes of thick egg custard, all coated in a light batter or with breadcrumbs. An Italian meal is also a well-balanced meal. For lunch, a first course of *minestra asciutta*, such as pasta or a risotto, is followed by a second course of a little meat or fish with sautéed vegetables or a crisp green salad. And then cheese and fruit. The evening meal usually starts with a soup, and then a *frittata*—Italian omelette—or a vegetable dish. Coffee may be served after the meal, at the table. It is usually served *espresso*, that is black without cream or milk.

Unfortunately in some industrial cities eating habits are slowly changing because of the pressures of our modern society. But if you want to taste the timeless joys of the Italian table, you can still do so by visiting regions such as Tuscany or Puglia or small towns all over the country, and by avoiding restaurants which cater for tourists and offer the international 'Italian' menu.

Where food is concerned I feel very patriotic. And for this reason, I have tried in this book to list recipes which exemplify the tradition of each region, despite the fact that the best of them are often unashamedly humble and unpretentious. These are dishes eaten every day in Italian homes, chosen, except for a few, with the busy cook in mind, as well as the availability of the ingredients here in Britain.

I hope you will enjoy preparing and eating them as much as I have enjoyed collecting them for you.

Piedmont

If you thought you were still in France while you made your way down from the Alps into the valleys of northern Italy, you would be excused: place names sound more French than Italian, French currency is widely accepted and many of the mountain dialects would be comprehensible to a French person but leave an Italian baffled. But it is differences in physical geography rather than of nationality that has led to variations in the cookery of this region.

In the mountains, patience and hard work have persuaded crops to grow at remarkable heights: a type of very small lettuce is cultivated just beneath the snow line and a little lower down endive and chicory can be found. Rye, barley and grapes are grown at a higher altitude than the summit of Ben Nevis and there is good pasturage at nearly 10,000 feet. In these remote places there are some fascinating foods, which have long been cultivated and eaten. One town produces edible thistles; in another, not far from the Provençal border, I once found a small market devoted exclusively to trading in empty chestnut shells.

Apart from these oddities, northern Piedmontese food has characteristics common to mountain cooking in all parts of the world. Uncomplicated, of heavy consistency and a little repetitive it often is, but above all it is always nourishing. Here you find hearty baked pasta dishes, such as *lasagne* and a type of *gnocchi* made from choux pastry. Boiled and roast meats of all sorts are extremely popular and so are sausages and ham. They are eaten with *polenta*, a type of porridge made with cornmeal, which was originally an Etruscan dish. *Polenta* is also excellent with poultry and game, of which there is no shortage. Vegetables play a relatively unimportant part in the cooking of the mountains. Nevertheless, beans, leeks, peppers, carrots, different types of lettuce, wild mushrooms and especially onions are quite common. Although there are several rich sweet puddings which are popular—that wonderful combination of chestnuts and cream, *monte bianco*, is the most famous—the commonest way of finishing a meal is with fruit.

In Turin and the rest of southern Piedmont, the cuisine owes much to Lombardy and to France and lacks a strong local identity. Although this is rice-growing territory—the eastern provinces of Vercelli and Novara produce three-quarters of Italy's total output—even risotto, the famous method of cooking rice, originates in Lombardy. Frogs thrive in the watery fields of the Po valley and are eaten in both Piedmont and in neighbouring Lombardy, fried in butter and stewed in white wine. Many cereals such as lentils and wheat, are grown here as are potatoes, which are made into *gnocchi*, many other varieties of vegetable and sugar beet. White truffles, the fungi which grow just under the surface soil, are the one great delicacy of southern Piedmont.

There are several genuine Piedmontese specialities, however. One is *grissini*, the long, narrow crusty fingers of wheatbread, which are delicious with such antipasti as truffles, ham and butter.

7

Another is *bagna cauda*, a 'hot bath' of olive oil and butter, garlic and finely chopped anchovy fillets, into which you dip raw vegetables. You should also try *fonduta*, a rich Piedmontese fondue made with *fontina*, a local cheese made from cow's milk.

Lombardy

Though Lombardy is dominated by Milan, Italy's financial capital, it remains basically an agricultural region—more wheat is produced per acre here than in any other Italian region. The importance of dairy farming is reflected in the cooking. Butter is the basic cooking fat, and the region produces some excellent cheeses. The best-known are *Gorgonzola* and *Bel Paese*, a mild soft cheese, readily available in Britain. Another local cheese is *taleggio*, which is made from cow's milk. Like a French brie, it ought to be eaten when it begins to ripen. Lombardy has its own version of Parmesan cheese, called *grana lodigiano*.

When in Milan I always go to the so-called Via dei Ghiottoni, 'the street of gourmets', which has food shops of every description. My favourite, called 'Peck', prides itself on the local veal it sells which is probably Italy's best and on its cheese section. Truffles, *prosciutto*, salami, *panettone*, nougat, freshly-made *ravioli* and *anolini* and all shapes, sizes and types of sausages are all spectacularly displayed. A rare type of salami called *felino*, made with pork, white wine and a touch of garlic, is one of the shop's specialities. You can also buy *bresaola*, which is fillet of beef cured in salt and then dried; it comes from the Valtellina, a valley north of Milan, and is eaten, cut into very thin slices, with olive oil, lemon juice and pepper.

Although Piedmont now grows more rice than Lombardy, far less is eaten there, and it is the Lombards who often refer to risotto as their 'national' dish. It is cooked slowly, like so many Milanese dishes, in a small amount of stock which is added gradually, and it is coloured with saffron. Saffron is included in many dishes and represents one of the few gastronomic traces of the Spanish who ruled Lombardy in the sixteenth and seventeenth centuries. Milan is, of course, also the home of *osso buco*, the wonderful stew of veal knuckles favoured especially for the bone marrow.

The Austrians occupied Lombardy for a long time and their influence can be detected in the Milanese preference to braise, stew or boil their meat and to spend hours at the stove to make sure that everything is cooked to perfection.

Veneto

The north-eastern corner of Italy comprises three provinces—Venetia Euganea, Venetia Gulia and Venetia Tridentina—which together form the region of Veneto. It is Venice in Venetia Euganea, once the heart of the world's greatest trading empire, which dominates the region's cooking. When its power was at its zenith, Venetian ships brought cargoes of exotic essences, spices and other foods unknown to the west from as far east as Syria and Turkey.

Gastronomic reminders of the great days of the empire which are common today include sole, cooked in sweet and sour sauce, and *fritelle*, little balls of candied fruit and sultanas fried in a sweet batter. Also rice with sultanas, pomegranates and turkey and even flowers, including violets, acacias and the flower of the courgette.

The fish market is one of the city's less publicised but most spectacular sights. Stall after stall is weighed down under the strain of endless varieties of fish: squids, shrimps, anchovies, clams, bass, scallops, crabs and many others provide a scene that is as decorative as it is mouthwatering.

The Venetians are not great lovers of pasta though they do enjoy their own version of *pasta fagioli*, pasta and bean soup. Rice is their favourite cereal, most popular when cooked with peas in a dish called *risi e bisi*.

It is hardly surprising that the city which introduced sugar to the rest of Europe should enjoy a host of sweet foods. A favourite moment for indulging this passion is in the middle of the morning when Venetians stop for their *ombrina*. This means 'little shade' and it refers to the awnings in St. Mark's Square, long gone, under which a glass of wine was drunk with a few sweet cornmeal biscuits called *le bisse*. The two eastern provinces, Venetia Gulia and Venetia Tridentina, have only been part of Italy since just after the Great War. Since the first area is closer to Yugoslavia and Hungary than the rest of Italy, there is a strong Slavic influence on the food. Venetia Gulia is the area known as Friuli. The people are poor and the local diet is very traditional, consisting of a lot of cereals, vegetables, pork and some game, as is so often the case in poor regions. Indeed, soups are staple food. The outstanding product of the region is a sweet fragrant ham made in the small town of San Daniele, near the Yugoslav border; the *prosciutto di San Daniele* is as highly regarded as that from Parma.

Liguria

Liguria is a narrow strip of land rising steeply out of the northern Mediterranean into the mountains behind. It is the home of the Italian riviera where the rich moor their boats and spend long, peaceful summers in the magnificent villas to be found in the hills all along the coastline.

Now the coast is sadly polluted. This is hardly surprising since the port of Genoa, in Liguria, is the largest in the Mediterranean. A few species of fish still survive , the best being the mussels, which used to be eaten raw with lemon and pepper. The mountains of Liguria are not suitable for the cultivation of crops or the raising of livestock, although they are dotted with olive groves and chestnut trees.

Much of the cooking of this region developed around its sea-faring menfolk, who were often at sea for weeks on end, and so food that would keep was prepared. This included salty meat, dried beans, pies and a type of hard biscuit which even the ships' mice were reluctant to nibble. (Pies from this region are still famous for the Ligurians are expert at packing as much nourishment as possible into a casing of pastry. Artichokes, Swiss chard and courgettes are the vegetables most frequently used as fillings.) It is from here too that *ravioli* originated. The name comes from the Genoese *robiole* meaning 'things of no importance', in this case leftovers which were stuffed into little envelopes of pasta for the men to take to sea with them.

When the sailors finally returned, immense and joyful feasts were prepared in their honour. The high spot of these occasions was often the appearance of the *torta pasqualina*, an elaborate spinach pie. Or possibly there was a *cappon magro*, an elaborate dome-shaped confection of boiled fish layered with different coloured, cooked vegetables.

Like so many seaside regions in Italy, Liguria has a delicious snack food which fishermen like to eat at odd times of the day either on land or in their boats. *Focaccia* is the Genoese pizza. It is a salted bread made with olive oil and a few other simple ingredients, perhaps local cheese or the pulp of freshly ground olives. Sometimes it is made with sage or finely sliced onions.

The region is best known now for spaghetti with *pesto*. It is a simple dish, but there are no two towns along the coastline which make it in exactly the same way. Some add ricotta, others lemon rind and often potatoes and French beans are included. But all are agreed that the essential ingredients are basil, olive oil, garlic and cheese.

Emilia-Romagna

This rich area of Italy, a large fertile triangular-shaped plain, borders the four northern regions and stretches right across to the Adriatic coast and south to Tuscany. The fertile soil in the region provides excellent pasture for cattle and this in turn means good milk, cream, butter, meat and cheeses.

At the northernmost point, near Ferrara, the greatest delicacy is eel. Every year thousands of them swim into prepared traps where they are suitably fattened, either for local consumption or export to other parts of Italy and abroad. When fresh, they are usually grilled. The others are roasted and then left to cool before being packed in vinegar.

Moving west one comes to Bologna, called *La Grassa* ('the fat'), a city famous for its meat sauces,

for many different baked pasta dishes, and, of course, *mortadella* sausage. An entire suckling pig may be used for the casing of a single mortadella sausage. Bologna is the home of the delicious *pasta tirata*, which is made with eggs. The variety of pasta you find in the region is endless—*tortelli, tortellini, cappelletti* ('little hats'), *tagliatelle, tagliolini* and *lasagne* are the most famous—all served with different stuffings or sauces.

Still further west, on the border of Lombardy, is Piacenza. There you can eat *bomba di riso* (rice bomb), a large semi-circular rice mould, which contains wild pigeons, onion, celery, carrot and dried wild mushrooms. The rice is cooked in white wine and the pigeon in red wine.

The centre of the classic *cucina emiliana* is Parma. *Prosciutto* and Parmesan are the province's most important products. Another speciality is tomato purée, usually associated, wrongly, with Naples and the south. It was originally produced here commercially at the beginning of this century and is now sold all over the world. And then there are the wild mushrooms, the fish from the Po, and game, such as pheasant, quail and hare.

Reggio Emilia is the home of Parmesan cheese. It became known as Parmesan—from Parma—because Reggio Emilia was once part of the dukedom of Parma.

Another speciality, this time from Modena, is *zampone*, from *zampa* which means paw; it is a large stuffed pig's trotter. Only the best parts of the pig are used as stuffing and the precise proportions of lean and fat are essential. *Zampone* is usually eaten with lentils.

Tuscany

Tuscany is the heart of Italy. Geographically central and one of the largest regions on the peninsula, its contribution to both Italian and European civilisation has been remarkable.

That Florence would eventually become the region's capital was perhaps inevitable as it was ruled by the richest and most powerful family of the Renaissance period, the Medici. They employed the best artists as well as the best cooks, both of whom were required to present work of great elaboration and beauty. In the case of food, however, their creative aspirations were restricted by laws which were periodically passed, limiting not only the number of guests permitted at a banquet but also the number of courses they were allowed to eat.

There is a disciplined and abstemious streak in Tuscans for which they are still famous and it is reflected in the way they eat. Elaborate cooking is alien to the way of life here. The food is simple and its excellence is reliant on the best ingredients. A good example is *bistecca alla fiorentina*, which consists simply of steaks from locally bred, two-year-old animals in their prime. The steaks must be grilled above burning chestnut wood sharply but only for a few minutes, salting the cooked side as it is turned over. Just before removing it from the grill a very small quantity of olive oil is rubbed on either side and then it is ready to eat, possibly with some fresh haricot beans, so beloved by all Tuscans. Other favourite vegetables are asparagus and artichokes.

Pheasants, hares, birds and even deer and wild boar can be found in the Tuscan hills. And, during the shooting season, when the hunters return home in the evening, with animals hanging from their belts, preparations are begun for cooking and devouring the bounty. Roasting is the most popular way of cooking game, and usually sweet-scented wild rosemary, the herb most loved by the Tuscans, is used to give the meat a characteristic aroma. Accompanying the meat will be the inevitable large, flat, round loaf of saltless bread, a little bit of which the Tuscans seem to put in their mouths with every forkful. There may also be a salad and there will certainly be some beans.

The Tuscans make one of the best *pecorino* cheeses in Italy. It is highly seasoned with a black crust and is a fine accompaniment to a glass of red wine. *Caciotta*, a semi-soft cheese made from sheep's or cow's milk, is also popular.

A delicious cake, eaten as a dessert, called *panforte* is the speciality of Siena. Rich in dried fruits, almonds and spices, its fame stretches all over Italy and it is a gastronomic must for any visitor to that uniquely beautiful mediaeval city. A lighter way to finish a meal, however, is with some *cantucci*, biscuits made in Prato, and a glass of *vin santo*.

Marche and Umbria

These two regions spread from the Adriatic coast through to the spectacularly beautiful Appenines of Umbria. It is a land laced with magnificent valleys, rivers, lakes and citadel towns perched on the tops of rocky mountains.

By the sea in the Marche region, is where most of the *Marchigiani* live, depending on the fishing industry for their livelihood. Nearly every town has its own carefully thought-out fish recipes which, in true provincial style, are the subject of much rivalry. For example, *brodetto*, the fish soup which the Ancient Greeks gave to the world, has an ever-varying recipe according to the locality and the content of the day's catch. What you are quite likely to find apart from fish, however, is white wine, onions, tomatoes, garlic and perhaps saffron.

Moving inland, we come to Umbria, which produces and consumes more meat per head than any other Italian region. There are cattle and pigs on the low ground, sheep and goats on the hills and, higher still, there is plenty of game. The local pork is of excellent quality and this is the only

meat which the Umbrians prepare elaborately. They use a variety of herbs, in particular thyme, rosemary and fennel to stuff a whole suckling pig which is then roasted.

Another of Umbria's best-known products is its truffles: the black truffles of Norcia and Spoleto. They are exquisite and even the French—usually a little snobbish about Italian food—import them.

This region also boasts some of Italy's finest freshwater fish from its fast-flowing mountain streams. In Lake Trasimeno, one of the largest in the country, is found a type of roach called *larca* which is delicious grilled and is well worth seeking out. There are also trout, perch and eels.

Lazio

Inevitably Rome dominates Lazio's cooking as it has its history for over 2000 years; but it is to the Etruscans that most of the credit for this varied cuisine must go.

To the Ancient Romans banqueting was a form of theatre, with food playing the principal part. For this purpose, it was elaborately dressed; birds, including flamingoes and peacocks, arrived at the dinner table in full plumage. Since there were no effective preserving methods, spices and essences, salt and honey were used in abundance to disguise the taste of food which might have gone bad.

Non-banqueting Romans—and there were plenty of them—had to rely on the very simplest foods. Many of them were shepherds, and lamb and mutton are both still popular in Roman cooking today. Sheep also provide milk and, of course, *pecorino* and *ricotta* cheeses. Between them, Lazio and Sardinia now produce half of Italy's entire output of *pecorino*, a hard cheese which is often used instead of Parmesan.

It seems almost impossible to find a type of food that the Romans dislike. Meat, fish, pasta, soups, vegetables and puddings are all equally good and cooked in wonderfully imaginative recipes. If you wanted a meat dish, you could choose from beef, veal, kid, poultry, pork, mutton, lamb and game. If you then choose pork from that list you would still have a wealth of options. Suckling pig, roasted on a spit, is extremely popular and may well mark a festive occasion. *Saltimbocca* (also known as *involtini*) combines *prosciutto* and veal in Marsala wine. *Prosciutto* again, this time with delicious young peas (another Roman passion), makes an exquisite pasta sauce called *piselli e prosciutto*.

The list of vegetables is no less extensive, the favourites being French beans, asparagus, artichokes, broccoli and *piselli novelli* (small young peas which are fresh and tender).

The Romans generally end their meal with fruit, of which water melon is one of the most popular. But you might well be served with *zuppa inglese*, neither a soup nor English, but perhaps so-called because of its similarity to trifle. This is accredited to the Roman cuisine, although it is made, with slight variations, everywhere south of the Po.

Abruzzi-Molise

There are two Italys, one northern and one southern. The northerners pride themselves on the technological progress they have made and the southerners claim to be more friendly. Abruzzi-Molise lies on the border of the two halves of Italy but technically is regarded as part of the south.

There are many poor people in this sparsely populated mountainous region and they frequently have to make do with a vegetable or egg dish as the main course. Onions, courgettes, celery, broccoli, artichokes, different types of beans, peppers, lentils and the ubiquitous tomato are the mainstays of the local cuisine.

The favourite meat is pork. It is roasted or made into sausages or preserved in other ways. There are countless local pork dishes often using bay leaves, garlic, chillies, rosemary and tomatoes. If a meat stew has been cooked, often its sauce will be served with pasta as a first course, and the meat eaten separately afterwards.

Kid and lamb are also popular. So too are the cows which graze on pastures as high as four thousand feet up. Cheeses are made from their milk, of which *pecorino* is the favourite, used both for cooking and for eating alone with bread.

By the sea—Abruzzi-Molise has a coastline stretching for a hundred miles—fish dominates the kitchen as you would expect, particularly octopus, squid, mackerel, anchovies and sardines. Pescara, which is the region's only sizeable port, enjoys lobster, while in the province of Teramo which borders Marche, boned and stuffed red mullet is the speciality. Fish is also commonly pickled and preserved in vinegar after being quickly fried. Inland there are many lakes and rivers where carp, tench and trout can be caught.

Campania

Campania includes the bustling city of Naples. This is the home of pasta, pizza and ice-cream. Surprisingly, however, none of them originated here. Both pasta and ice-cream came via Sicily. Indeed the Sicilians used to refer to the Neapolitans as 'leaf-eaters' because, lacking pasta, their diet was based on vegetables. However, pasta has now become their favourite food.

The pizza started life as the staple ancient Roman breakfast and it is still fundamentally the same round slice of bread with a raised edge to hold in some sauce. Various shapes and sizes are popular now: it may be small (*pizzetta*, in which case it becomes a snack), or it may be folded over to trap the filling (*calzone*), but it is normally the size of a large plate. Though the variations of pizza filling are endless, the cheese used is

normally *mozzarella* which comes, ideally, from the milk of buffaloes. But since the demand for *mozzarella* is so great and the number of buffaloes has dwindled, it is commonly made from cow's milk. It is a very bland cheese and should really be eaten on the day it is made when it is at its best. The Neapolitans are very fond of *mozzarella* and eat it in a variety of ways, sometimes fried, or in a salad or simply on its own with salt, pepper and olive oil.

There is a scarcity of meat in this region which is made up for by the many varieties of fish. Mussels, in particular, are extremely popular and are often added to dishes using other fish, pasta sauces and even toppings for pizzas.

Although generally uncomplicated eaters, the Neapolitans do allow themselves scope for elaboration when it comes to sweets and desserts: pies, flans, cakes, pastries and above all ice-cream can be found throughout the region.

Puglia

Puglia, the richest of Italy's three southern states, is nicknamed 'the granary of Italy', for its unrivalled production of durum wheat, the chief ingredient of pasta.

Apart from the game to be found in the forests which cover the mountains in the spur of Italy's 'boot', there is little meat in this region. Pasta consequently is frequently the main course of a meal and the making and cooking of it and preparation of its sauce is treated with great seriousness.

Bread is, if anything, even better loved than pasta. It is still made by the more conscientious housewife in the home. As in other parts of Italy, the favourite method of serving bread is with oil, tomatoes and onions.

Puglia's long coastline is particularly well-endowed with various species of fish. The method employed to cultivate oysters in Taranto is still the same as that used by the Romans. The oysters attach themselves to frames which are then moved from a lagoon where the water is less salty, to a sheltered area of sea where there is more for them to eat. The whole process takes several months, but the combination of brackish and salt water provides perfect conditions for the breeding of delicious oysters.

The landscape in the southern part of Puglia is full of vineyards and orchards, and dotted with curious little constructions called *trulli*. These one-roomed conical dwellings made of stone, which still house peasant families, look like huge white-washed bee-hives. Inside you may well find tomatoes strung across the ceiling to dry and bunches of onions and garlic.

While in Lecce, which lies at the very heel of the peninsular, one of the most characteristic sights is the endless rows of huge and ancient olive trees which sometimes fill the entire landscape and produce the regions characteristic olive oil.

11

Basilicata and Calabria

These two regions which share the foot of the Italian boot with Puglia are Italy's poorest. Calabria has not always been so badly off.

Basilicata has an unrivalled history of anonymity, partly explained by its geography. The mountains stretch right down to the sea, making the coastline relatively inaccessible and thus preventing the establishment of fishing communities.

Calabria is also mountainous—often it is not until June that the snow finally disappears from the vast central plateau known as Sila. But it is full of game and exquisitely tasty small wild mushrooms. Fish, too, is important to the diet of Calabrians who enjoy a wide variety of species, although tuna and swordfish are, as in Sicily, the pick of the catch.

In both of these regions the most striking feature of local cooking is its simplicity. The tourists are fed the standard, Naples-orientated food, while the simple vegetable and pasta diet of those who produce it can only be found in the home. Of the little meat that is produced, pork is the most important and there is also some kid and lamb. The sausages in both Calabria and Basilicata, are highly seasoned and hot. Both regions, in fact, are very much given to hotly peppered food, whether it be a pasta or a vegetable soup or a combination of the two. One course usually has to suffice here, with perhaps a little cheese and home-grown fruit to follow. To help combat the monotony, pasta comes in countless shapes and sizes, although it is most commonly served in a sauce containing garlic, onions, tomatoes and olive oil. A generous sprinkling of *pecorino* adds nourishment and substance.

Aubergines are very popular in all of southern Italy and nowhere more so than in these two regions. Stuffed or fried, they are prepared with all sorts of combinations of the same ingredients: eggs, mushrooms, *pecorino*, breadcrumbs, parsley, garlic and, of course, tomatoes, hot red chillies and olive oil.

Basilicata tends to prefer chillies rather than pepper to strengthen its food—they are often used in such quantities that you cannot taste anything else. However the highly-spiced sausages of this region are considered so good that in Milan *basilicata* is often used as a byword for any good spicy sausages. There is also an excellent smoked mountain *prosciutto*. In the higher reaches of Basilicata, beyond the chestnut trees which occupy so much of the middle level of the countryside, there is a lot of game, including wild boar. If you are lucky you may even see a wolf, for this is one of the very few corners of western Europe where this animal still exists. Farther down, the soil is not especially good, but olive trees and above all citrus fruits are successfully grown.

In Calabria, on the other hand, there are considerable stretches of rich agricultural land, much of which is covered by citrus trees. The bergamot tree also grows here. Its oil is used for making perfume and skin lotions and Calabria has a world monopoly in this commodity.

Sicily

Sicilian food owes much to the many and varied foreign powers who have occupied her over the centuries. For example, the Normans contributed *stoccafisso*, salt cod. While the Saracens introduced a taste for sweet food which, likewise, is now part of all traditional Italian cookery. They also introduced sorbet (from which ice-cream was soon to follow), nougat, candied fruit and marzipan. *Cassata*, also of Saracen origin, contains ricotta cheese, first made by the Greeks.

Despite inclement weather and soil conditions, durum wheat is grown extensively inland and much of it is made into pasta. Following pasta come the citrus fruits which are grown in greater quantity here than anywhere else in Italy. Almond and fig trees are another common sight.

As with all of the poor regions of the south, the excellence of the vegetables makes up for the lack of meat. A visitor to Palermo would be unwise not to visit the market, where cascades of red, green and yellow peppers alternate on the stalls with broccoli, courgettes, aubergines and lettuce.

King amongst Sicilian fish is the tuna, closely followed by the swordfish. There are also the more common types of fish which are found all over the Mediterranean, including anchovies and sardines, the latter being very popular with pasta.

Sardinia

Sardinia is a thinly populated island which has plenty of room for pigs, goats and sheep to wander freely. This means good cheese, the most common being a hard 'pecorino' made from sheep's milk.

The long dry Sardinian summers are ideal for growing durum wheat, which the Sardinians, rather than use it for pasta, prefer to make bread from which they bake with religious reverence. There is bread for every occasion, often flavoured with herbs or onions.

Stuffed pancakes, called *empanadas*, are a legacy left by the Spanish invaders of the eighteenth century. They are filled with meat or vegetables and are served either hot or cold.

Game is a very important feature of local cooking. Deer, hares, wild boars, rabbits and birds of all sorts are extremely popular, and when it comes to cooking game, nobody takes more care than the Sardinian. Leaves from the myrtle bushes that grow everywhere give roasts a distinct flavour and they are cooked slowly, with plenty of herbs, over an open wood fire.

The cakes and pastries, many of them containing almonds and lemon or orange peel, are particularly delicious.

ANTIPASTI

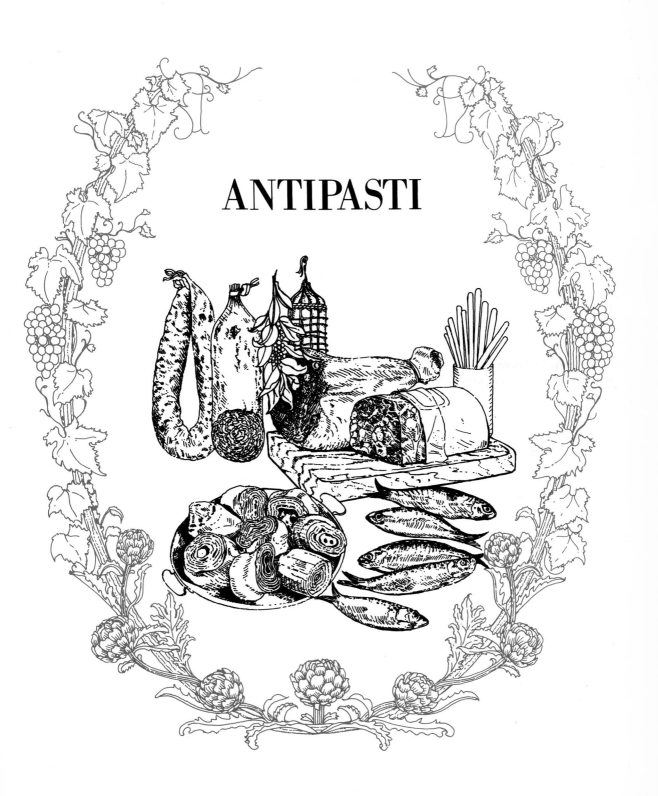

Uova Sode alla Pugliese   *Hard-boiled eggs from Puglia*

PUGLIA

The poverty of southern Italy is reflected in many of its dishes. This one, however, is one of the tastiest and most unusual ways to serve hard-boiled eggs. It makes an unusual summer hors d'oeuvres, served with large black olives.

Preparation time: 15 minutes
Cooking time: 10 minutes
Serves: 6

45 ml/3 tablespoons olive oil
15 ml/1 tablespoon wine vinegar
½ small fresh chilli, seeded and chopped
30 ml/2 tablespoons chopped fresh parsley
1 garlic clove, very finely chopped
60 ml/4 level tablespoons fresh breadcrumbs
salt
6 eggs, hard-boiled and cut in half, lengthwise
black or green olives

Heat the oil and vinegar in a small frying pan, add the chilli, parsley and garlic and sauté for 1 minute. Add the breadcrumbs and sauté for 2 to 3 minutes, stirring all the time, until just golden. Add salt to taste. Pile 10 ml/2 level teaspoons of the mixture on top of each egg half.

Serve cold with black or green olives.

Insalata di Frutti di Mare   *Seafood salad*

CAMPANIA

Try your own variation on seafood salad by using whatever types of fish or shell-fish you find fresh in the market.

Preparation time: 30 minutes plus 2 hours
   marinating
Cooking time: 35 minutes
Serves: 4

350 g/12 oz squid
750 g/1½ lb or 1·1 litres/2 pints mussels
225 ml/8 fl oz olive oil
1 onion
1 bay leaf
salt and freshly ground black pepper
350 g/12 oz prawns
15 ml/1 tablespoon wine vinegar
350 g/12 oz shelled scallops (about 7)
100 g/4 oz shelled shrimps
60 ml/4 tablespoons lemon juice
30 ml/2 level tablespoons capers
45 ml/3 tablespoons chopped fresh parsley
1 small garlic clove, finely chopped
black olives

Clean the squid following the instructions on page 89.

To clean the mussels, put them in a sink and scrub them thoroughly with a hard brush, scraping off any barnacles with a knife. Discard any mussels which are not tightly closed and put the rest in a colander under cold running water. Leave them for about 20 minutes.

Put the cleaned mussels in a large saucepan with 30 ml/ 2 tablespoons of the olive oil and 150 ml/¼ pint water. Cover the pan and cook over high heat for 5 to 10 minutes until the mussels open, shaking the pan during the cooking. Then lift them out of the pan, shell the mussels, place in a salad bowl and set aside.

Add 1·75 litres/3 pints of water, the onion, bay leaf and 5 ml/1 teaspoon salt to the mussel liquid. Bring to the boil and then add the squid. Simmer, covered, for 10 minutes.

Wash the prawns in cold water and add them to the squid. Cover and cook for about 10 minutes, until the squid are cooked and can be easily pierced with a fork. Drain and set aside, reserving the liquid for a fish soup.

Bring 900 ml/1½ pints of water to the boil. Add the vinegar, a little salt and scallops, cook for 3 minutes.

Peel the prawns and cut them into rounds 1 cm/½ inch thick. Cut the squid into strips of the same width and the scallops into 0·5-cm/¼-inch cubes. Add all the seafood to the mussels in the bowl together with the shrimps.

In a small bowl mix together the remaining oil, lemon juice, capers, parsley, garlic and pepper. Pour the sauce over the seafood and toss gently.

Allow the fish salad to stand for at least 2 hours before serving garnished with black olives.

Pomodori Ripieni di Riso, surrounded by Uova Sode alla Pugliese and, right, Insalata di Frutti di Mare

Pomodori Ripieni di Riso *Tomatoes stuffed with rice*

LAZIO

Dishes of lusciously-coloured stuffed veg-etables are one of the joys of Italian cook-ing, and always among them are tomatoes. Often they are served raw, stuffed simply with tuna mixed with mayonnaise as part of an antipasto. In this recipe from Rome, the stuffed tomatoes are baked with tiny pieces of potatoes which turn crisp and golden and add an interesting contrast to the dish. Try to get the big knobbly tomatoes, which have more flavour.

Preparation time: 15 minutes
Cooking time: 45 minutes
Oven temperature: 200°C, 400°F,
  Gas Mark 6
Serves: 6

6 large tomatoes, each weighing about
  200 g/7 oz, ripe but firm
60 ml/4 level tablespoons long-grain rice
60 ml/4 tablespoons olive oil
1 garlic clove, finely chopped
a few fresh basil leaves, or 10 ml/2 teaspoons
  oregano
15 ml/1 tablespoon chopped fresh parsley
salt and freshly ground black pepper
1 large potato, cut into very small cubes

Cut the top from each tomato, and chop it roughly. Scoop the flesh and seeds out of the tomatoes and purée them and the chopped tops through a food-mill or a sieve. Put the purée into a bowl and add the rice, 45 ml/3 table-spoons of the oil, the garlic, basil or oregano, parsley and salt and pepper. Mix thoroughly. Sprinkle the inside of the tomatoes with salt and fill them with the mixture.

Put the tomatoes in a buttered ovenproof dish, in which they will fit comfortably, but not too loosely.

Place a few potato cubes in between each tomato and sprinkle the dish with salt and pepper. Pour over the remaining oil and bake in the oven for about 45 minutes, until tender.

Serve hot.

Fritto Misto *Mixed fried foods*

EMILIA-ROMAGNA

In Italy *fritto misto* is often served as a complete meal, just like the example I have given here, which is for 4 servings. You would begin with a first course, the *Stecchini di Mortadella e Formaggio*, followed by the meat and vegetable dishes. You could finish with apple fritters but perhaps that would be too much!

Alternatively, these dishes make excellent first courses for dinner parties or they may be served hot or cold for buffets and fork luncheons. At their best served immediately after cooking, they nevertheless heat up satisfactorily in a cool oven. The preparation and cooking times given are for a complete meal.

Preparation time: 1 hour plus 1 hour standing for the pastella
Cooking time: 30 minutes
Serves: 4 as a complete meal and 12–15 as appetisers

The coatings
The foods to be fried are first coated in either batter (*pastella*) or in an egg and breadcrumb mixture (*uova e pangrattato*). Heat the oil—I use sunflower or corn oil—until it will turn a crust of bread golden in 1 minute. It should come about 3 cm/1¼ inches up the sides of a deep fat fryer. Salt the food before adding to the pan and do not put in too many items at one time. The oil may be strained and re-used for two or three meals before discarding.

Pastella *Italian batter*
2 eggs
pinch of salt
100 g/4 oz plain flour, sifted
30 ml/2 tablespoons vegetable oil
90 ml/6 tablespoons water

Lightly beat the eggs with the pinch of salt. Add the flour, a little at a time, beating constantly. Then pour in the oil and the water. Beat well and allow to rest for 1 hour.

Uova e Pangrattato *Egg and breadcrumbs*
2 eggs
pinch of salt
200 g/7 oz fine fresh dried breadcrumbs

Lightly beat the eggs with the salt in a large bowl. Place the breadcrumbs in another large bowl. The items to be coated are dipped first in the eggs and then in breadcrumbs.

Cotolettine di Carne *Deep-fried meat slices*
350 g/12 oz veal escalopes or turkey escalopes, very finely sliced
350 g/12 oz pig's liver, very finely sliced
egg and breadcrumb coating

Cut the meat and the liver into 5-cm/2-inch squares. Dip each piece into the egg and then coat with the breadcrumbs, patting the crumbs down with your hands. Fry for 2 to 3 minutes, turning once, until crisp and brown. Do not overcook. Drain on absorbent kitchen paper.

Verdure Fritte *Fried vegetables*
Choose a selection of these vegetables and coat as directed in the method.

225 g/8 oz cauliflower florets, fennel cut into wedges, tomatoes cut into wedges or large mushroom caps
egg and breadcrumb coating

Cook the cauliflower florets or fennel in salted boiling water for 5 minutes. Drain well and cut the larger cauliflower florets in half. Dip all the vegetables in the egg and then the breadcrumbs and fry in batches for 2 to 3 minutes until crisp and golden. Drain on absorbent kitchen paper.

225 g/8 oz small courgettes or aubergines
Italian batter

Cut the courgettes into lengthways slices, about 0·5 cm/¼ inch thick. Dip into the batter and fry in the hot oil for 3 to 4 minutes, turning once, until the batter is crisp and golden. Transfer to absorbent kitchen paper.

Cut the aubergines into slices and leave to stand sprinkled with salt in a colander to sweat for at least 30 minutes. Dry them well before coating and frying as for courgettes.

Stecchini di Mortadella e Formaggio   *Skewers of mortadella and cheese*

100 g/4 oz Gruyère or other hard cheese
175 g/6 oz mortadella, in one piece
2 thick slices of white bread
90 ml/6 tablespoons milk
egg and breadcrumb coating

Cut the cheese, the mortadella and the bread into 1-cm/ ½-inch cubes. Slide a cube of each ingredient on to a cocktail stick. Warm the milk in a saucepan and dip each skewer into it. Then coat with the egg and then the breadcrumbs. Fry for 2 to 3 minutes until golden. Drain on absorbent kitchen paper.

Crostini alla Chiantigiana   *Pâté from Chianti*

TUSCANY

We once had a house in Chianti and used to spend long holidays there. The gastronomic highlight of our stay was always lunch with the Restis, a local family who live in part of an eleventh century fortified farmstead on the top of one of the most beautiful hills in Tuscany. We had many meals there. These *crostini* were always served as an antipasto, together with pieces of the local *pecorino*, a dry, well-seasoned cheese; they were washed down with a glass of *Vinsanto*, a semi-sweet fortified white wine, which is a Tuscan speciality. Then would follow a great dish of pasta and a chicken from their back garden, both cooked with different sauces every time we went. The chicken was accompanied by chips—they were the lightest and least fatty chips I ever had—and a basil-flavoured salad. *Zuppa inglese*, English trifle, made I think in honour of my English husband and our children, would end the meal.

This is Anna Resti's recipe for *crostini*.

Preparation time: 15 minutes
Cooking time: 35 minutes
Serves: 6

225 g/8 oz chicken livers
45 ml/3 tablespoons olive oil
50 g/2 oz butter
½ celery stick, very finely chopped
½ carrot, very finely chopped
1 small onion, very finely chopped
15 ml/1 tablespoon chopped fresh parsley
45 ml/3 tablespoons dry white wine
7·5 ml/½ level tablespoon tomato purée,
  diluted in 50 ml/2 fl oz warm water
salt and freshly ground black pepper
15 ml/1 level tablespoon capers, chopped
1 small garlic clove, chopped
2 anchovy fillets, chopped
toasted French bread

Remove all the fat from the chicken livers. Wash, dry well and cut into small pieces. Put the oil and half the butter in a saucepan and, when hot, add the celery, carrot, onion and parsley and cook for 5 to 10 minutes until soft. Add the chicken livers and cook very gently—they must *not* fry— until they have lost their raw colour. Pour over the wine, raise the heat and reduce until nearly all the wine has evaporated. Lower the heat and add the diluted tomato purée, a little salt and plenty of pepper and simmer gently, covered, for 20 minutes.

When the chicken livers are ready, remove the pan from the heat and add the capers, garlic, anchovies and the remaining butter. Mix until the butter has melted and been incorporated and then coarsely purée the mixture. Return to the saucepan and cook slowly for 2 minutes, stirring constantly.

Serve the crostini either warm or cold, spread over toasted French bread.

Tagliatelle con Sugo di Cipolle   *Tagliatelle with onion sauce*

EMILIA-ROMAGNA

This delicious onion sauce turns golden and looks beautiful tossed in plain, rather than green, tagliatelle.

Preparation: 15 minutes plus about 1 hour
  for pasta making
Cooking time: 45 minutes
Serves: 4 as a first course

50 g/2 oz butter
45 ml/3 tablespoons vegetable oil
3 large onions, finely chopped
5 ml/1 level teaspoon flour
1·25 ml/¼ level teaspoon meat extract,
  dissolved in 30 ml/2 tablespoons warm
  water
salt and freshly ground black pepper
tagliatelle made with 3 eggs, 300 g/11 oz
  flour (see page 139) or 400 g/14 oz bought
  tagliatelle
50 g/2 oz freshly grated Parmesan cheese

Melt 25 g/1 oz of the butter with the oil in a small heavy saucepan. Add the onions and cook over very low heat for 10 minutes, stirring frequently. Add the flour, meat extract, salt and pepper. Stir well, and press the onions against the sides of the pan with a spoon to release their juice.

Cover the pan and cook over very low heat for at least 30 minutes, until the onion is reduced to pulp. Then uncover, raise the heat and cook until the sauce is a rich golden colour.

Have a large saucepan of salted water boiling rapidly, and just before the sauce is ready, put in the pasta. Cook until *al dente*, firm to the bite.

Drain and toss the pasta with the remaining butter. Add the onion sauce and the Parmesan. Mix well and serve at once.

Tagliolini con Salsa di Porri   *Thin tagliatelle with leeks*

VALLE D'AOSTA, PIEDMONT

In Biella, one of the most unremarkable provincial towns in Italy, I once had an extraordinary pasta dish. It contained a touch of curry powder, which is certainly not an Italian ingredient. However, I think that this union of Indian and Italian cooking is a great success.

Ideally this recipe should be made with home-made pasta, *tagliolini* being a narrower version of *tagliatelle*. However, the sauce is very good with bought thin spaghetti.

Preparation time: 15 minutes plus 1 hour
  for pasta making
Cooking time: 35 minutes
Serves: 4 as a first course

100 g/4 oz butter
1 kg/2 lb leeks, white parts only, cut into
  thin rings
5 ml/1 level teaspoon curry powder
100 ml/4 fl oz home-made meat stock (see
  page 138)
salt
tagliatelle made with 3 eggs and 300 g/
  11 oz flour (see page 139) or 400 g/14 oz
  bought tagliatelle
30 ml/2 tablespoons single cream
50 g/2 oz freshly grated Parmesan cheese

In a large frying pan, melt the butter and add the leeks. Stir for 30 seconds, then add the curry powder and the stock and cook, over very low heat for 30 minutes. Taste and adjust the seasoning. While the leeks are cooking, drop the pasta into rapidly boiling salted water. Remember that if you are using fresh home-made tagliatelle it will only take 30 seconds to cook. Drain when still very *al dente*, firm to the bite, reserving 45 ml/3 tablespoons of the water in which the pasta has boiled.

Add the tagliatelle to the leeks in the frying pan. Add the cream, half the cheese and the reserved cooking liquid. Mix thoroughly and cook over low heat for 2 minutes.

Serve at once from the pan, with the remaining Parmesan in a bowl.

Tagliatelle con Prosciutto e Piselli _Tagliatelle with prosciutto and peas_

TUSCANY

Two locally produced ingredients are combined to produce this wonderful sauce which tastes as good with spaghetti as it does with tagliatelle.

Preparation time: 8 minutes plus 1 hour for pasta making
Cooking time: 10 minutes
Serves: 4 as a first course

100 g/4 oz prosciutto, the fat and lean separated
100 g/4 oz butter
½ small onion, very finely chopped
100 g/4 oz peas, cooked
tagliatelle made with 3 eggs, 300 g/11 oz flour (see page 139) or 400 g/14 oz bought tagliatelle
30 ml/2 tablespoons single cream
50 g/2 oz freshly grated Parmesan cheese
salt and freshly ground black pepper

Chop the prosciutto fat finely. Cut the lean prosciutto into matchsticks. In a large frying pan, melt the butter and fry the prosciutto fat and the onion for about 3 minutes, until soft. Add the lean prosciutto and the peas and cook for 5 minutes.

Meanwhile drop the tagliatelle into rapidly boiling salted water and cook until _al dente_, firm to the bite.

Drain and add to the prosciutto and peas in the frying pan. Stir well and then add the cream and half the Parmesan. Toss gently for 30 seconds, season well and serve at once, with the remaining Parmesan in a separate bowl.

Tagliatelle con Prosciutto e Piselli

Zucchine Ripiene *Stuffed courgettes*

EMILIA-ROMAGNA

These courgettes are hollowed into 'tumbler' shapes, rather than slit as they often are for stuffing. It makes an ideal dish for vegetarians and may be served either hot or cold—both are equally good.

Preparation time: 20 minutes (plus 30 minutes draining)
Cooking time: 40 minutes
Serves: 4

8 small or 6 large courgettes, with the ends sliced off and cut into 5-cm/2-inch pieces
salt and freshly ground black pepper
45 ml/3 tablespoons vegetable oil
1 onion, very finely chopped
30 ml/2 tablespoons tomato purée diluted in 250 ml/9 fl oz water
30 ml/2 tablespoons chopped fresh parsley
1 garlic clove, very finely sliced
50 g/2 oz fresh dried breadcrumbs
50 g/2 oz freshly grated Parmesan cheese
1 egg

With a vegetable peeler, hollow the courgette pieces out, leaving a base. Be careful not to perforate the outside wall. Sprinkle the courgette 'tumblers' with salt and leave to drain for 30 minutes. Chop the pulp finely and put into a bowl.

Heat the vegetable oil with the onion in a frying pan large enough to accommodate all the courgettes in a single layer. Gently fry the onion for about 5 minutes, until very soft. Add the tomato purée and cook slowly over low heat for 10 minutes.

While the tomato sauce is cooking, add the parsley, garlic, breadcrumbs, Parmesan, egg, salt and pepper to the courgette pulp, and mix thoroughly with a spoon or with your hands. Dry the courgette 'tumblers' thoroughly and fill with this mixture.

Place the courgettes on the tomatoes in the frying pan, spoon a little sauce over each of them, and lower the heat. Cook, covered, for about 40 minutes, until tender. Baste occasionally during the cooking. Taste the tomato sauce and adjust seasonings.

Leave to settle for 5 minutes before serving or allow to cool completely and serve at room temperature, but not chilled.

Farfalle al Sugo di Verdure *Noodle bows in ratatouille sauce*

LIGURIA

This creamy sauce for pasta is quite easy to prepare, but it must be made with very fresh vegetables.

Preparation time: 15 minutes (plus 30 minutes to prepare the aubergine)
Cooking time: 1 hour
Serves: 6 as a first course

1 small aubergine, peeled and cut into small cubes
salt and freshly ground black pepper
1 garlic clove, very finely sliced
90 ml/6 tablespoons olive oil
2 small courgettes, cut into small cubes
1 small pepper, seeded and cut into small cubes
397-g/14-oz can plum tomatoes, with their juice, roughly chopped
500 g/1 lb noodle bows or other short pasta

Put the aubergine into a colander, sprinkle with salt and leave to drain for at least 30 minutes. Rinse and pat dry with absorbent kitchen paper.

Fry the garlic in 60 ml/4 tablespoons of the oil in a saucepan for about 2 minutes, until the garlic is just coloured. Add the cubed vegetables and sauté for 5 minutes, stirring frequently. Add the tomatoes, salt and pepper and cook, over moderate heat, for 1 hour, stirring occasionally.

Purée the sauce through a food-mill, liquidiser or a food processor and add the remaining oil. Keep warm while the pasta is cooking.

Put the pasta into rapidly boiling salted water and cook until *al dente*, firm to the bite. Drain, pour into a heated serving dish and spoon over the sauce. Serve immediately.

Funghi alla Palermitana *Baked mushrooms from Palermo*

SICILY

These mushrooms look pretty served in individual cocotte dishes, although traditionally they are served in one dish.

Preparation time: 20 minutes
Cooking time: 15 minutes
Oven temperature: 200°C, 400°F,
*   Gas Mark 6*
Serves: 6

500 g/1 lb mushrooms, thickly sliced
60 ml/4 tablespoons olive oil
1 garlic clove, finely chopped
2 anchovy fillets, very finely chopped
1-cm/½-inch piece of fresh chilli, seeded
*   and very finely chopped*
30 ml/2 tablespoons chopped fresh parsley
10 ml/2 teaspoons lemon juice
salt
45 ml/3 level tablespoons fresh dried
*   breadcrumbs*
15 g/½ oz butter

Place the mushrooms, oil, garlic, anchovies, chilli, parsley, lemon juice and salt in a bowl and mix together well. Adjust the seasoning. Grease six cocotte dishes, fill them with the mushroom mixture and sprinkle with the breadcrumbs. Put a knob of butter on top of each cocotte, and bake in the oven for about 15 minutes, until a light crust is formed.

Timpano Settecentesco di Maccheroni e Pomodori
Baked macaroni and tomatoes

CAMPANIA

This eighteenth-century recipe from Naples was given to me by my Neapolitan grandfather, who loved the traditional food of his native city and wanted it to survive for future generations. Use only good quality ingredients for the best results.

Preparation time: 15 minutes
Cooking time: 20 minutes
Oven temperature: 200°C, 400°F,
*   Gas Mark 6*
Serves: 4 as a first course

400 g/14 oz cut tubular pasta, such as
*   penne or macaroni*
225 ml/8 fl oz olive oil
30 ml/2 level tablespoons fresh dried
*   breadcrumbs*
60 ml/4 tablespoons freshly grated
*   Parmesan cheese*
2·5 ml/½ teaspoon oregano
1-cm/½-inch piece of fresh chilli, seeded and
*   finely chopped*
550 g/1¼ lb tomatoes, skinned and each cut
*   into 4 slices*
salt and freshly ground black pepper

Cook the pasta in a saucepan of rapidly boiling salted water for 5 minutes after the water has come back to the boil. Drain and return it to the saucepan. Add the olive oil (reserving 30 ml/2 tablespoons), the breadcrumbs, Parmesan, oregano and chilli and toss well.

Butter a deep ovenproof dish and cover the bottom with some tomato slices, reserving the outer slices for the top, and sprinkle with salt and pepper. Cover with half of the pasta, another third of the tomatoes and then a layer of the remaining pasta. Cover with the reserved outer slices of the tomatoes, the round part upwards.

Pour over the remaining oil, sprinkle with salt and pepper and cover the dish with foil. Bake in the oven for 10 minutes. Remove the foil and bake for a further 10 minutes. Put the dish under the grill for 2 to 3 minutes until the tops of the tomatoes are just charred. Allow to settle for 5 minutes before serving.

Spaghetti alla Puttanesca

Spaghetti with tomatoes, anchovy fillets and black olives

LAZIO

This very old recipe from Rome has its origins in one of the poorest and oldest districts of the city, the Trastevere, the traditional haunt of Roman prostitutes. Its name (*puttana* means prostitute in Italian) certainly owes something to the fact it is a hot sauce quickly prepared!

Preparation time: 10 minutes
Cooking time: 10 minutes
Serves: 4 as a first course

500 g/1 lb tomatoes, skinned, seeded and cut into thin strips, or 397-g/14-oz can plum tomatoes, drained and roughly chopped
45 ml/3 tablespoons olive oil
400 g/14 oz spaghetti
salt
50 g/2 oz butter
2·5-cm/1-inch piece of fresh chilli, seeded and finely chopped
8 anchovy fillets, chopped
2 garlic cloves, very finely sliced
100 g/4 oz large black olives, stoned and sliced
15 ml/1 level tablespoon capers
15 ml/1 tablespoon chopped fresh parsley

If you are using fresh tomatoes, fry in a saucepan in 7·5 ml/½ tablespoon of the oil for 5 minutes. If you are using canned tomatoes, fry for 3 minutes.

Drop the pasta into rapidly boiling salted water and cook until *al dente*, firm to the bite.

While the pasta is cooking, put the remaining oil, butter, chilli, anchovy fillets and garlic in a large frying pan and cook for 1 minute, mashing the anchovies to a paste with a fork. Add the tomato sauce, olives and capers and cook for 2 to 3 minutes, stirring frequently.

Drain the spaghetti, turn it into the frying pan, and add the parsley. Fry for 1 minute, tossing the pasta all the time. Serve at once from the pan.

Spaghetti alla Puttanesca

Spaghetti Aglio, Olio e Prezzemolo

Spaghetti with garlic, parsley and oil sauce

LAZIO

A very simple Roman sauce. It is best to use *spaghettini*, which are very thin spaghetti, although ordinary spaghetti also gives good results.

Preparation time: 5 minutes
Cooking time: 10 minutes
Serves: 4 as a first course

100 ml/4 fl oz olive oil
3 garlic cloves, very finely chopped
2·5-cm/1-inch piece of fresh chilli, seeded
    and very finely chopped
salt
400 g/14 oz spaghettini
45 ml/3 tablespoons chopped fresh parsley

Heat the oil in a large frying pan and sauté the garlic, chillies and a little salt, stirring frequently, until the garlic cloves are a golden brown. Be careful not to burn the garlic.

Meanwhile, cook the pasta in rapidly boiling salted water, until it is *al dente*, firm to the bite. Drain the pasta, add it to the frying pan and toss it over heat for 1 minute. Add the parsley, mix thoroughly and serve immediately.

Spaghetti con Cozze e Sugo di Pomodoro

Spaghetti with mussels and tomato sauce

CAMPANIA

This is a perfect *ménage à trois* of the three greatest Neapolitan products and is an easy recipe to prepare. Do not use mussels which are already shelled or the kind preserved in vinegar.

Preparation time: 45 minutes
Cooking time: 30 minutes
Serves: 4 as first course

2·25 litres/2 quarts or 1·25–1·5 kg/2½–3 lb
    mussels in their shells
75 ml/3 fl oz olive oil
1 garlic clove, finely chopped
30 ml/2 tablespoons chopped fresh parsley
500 g/1 lb tomatoes, skinned, or
    397-g/14-oz can plum tomatoes, with
    their juice
salt and freshly ground black pepper
400 g/14 oz spaghettini (thin spaghetti)

To clean the mussels, put them in a sink and scrub them thoroughly with a hard brush, scraping off any barnacles with a knife. Discard any mussels which are not tightly closed and put the rest in a colander under cold running water. Leave them for about 20 minutes.

When they are clean, place the mussels in a large saucepan. Cover and cook over high heat until the mussels are open, shaking the pan occasionally. Remove the mussel meat from the shells and discard the shells. Strain the liquid left in the pan through a piece of muslin or absorbent kitchen paper and reduce it over high heat. You should have no more than 200 ml/7 fl oz.

Heat the oil, garlic and 15 ml/1 tablespoon of the parsley in a saucepan until the garlic is just coloured. Add the strained liquid and turn up the heat high, further reducing the liquid by half. Purée the tomatoes and add to the pan. Add plenty of pepper. Cook, uncovered, over moderate heat for 15 minutes.

Meanwhile drop the pasta into rapidly boiling salted water and cook until *al dente*, firm to the bite.

Just before the spaghetti is ready, add the mussels to the sauce. Turn the heat to very low and mix. The mussels must not cook, they should only get warm. Adjust the seasoning.

Drain the spaghetti, turn into a heated dish and cover with the sauce. Sprinkle with the remaining parsley and serve at once.

Spaghettini in Bianco con le Vongole *Thin spaghetti with clams*

CAMPANIA

This sauce should be made with small clams which are seldom found in Britain. You can sometimes find them at fish markets, otherwise use clams preserved in salted water and sold in jars or cans (not the kind in vinegar). The sauce can also be made with cockles, which, however, contain a lot of grit and must be cleaned very thoroughly.

Preparation time: 30 minutes, if fresh clams are used; 10 minutes, if canned clams are used
Cooking time: 5 minutes
Serves: 4 as a first course

1·25 litres/2 pints or 750 g/1½ lb clams in their shells or two 290-g/10·2-oz cans baby clams in brine
400 g/14 oz thin spaghetti
45 ml/3 tablespoons olive oil
2 garlic cloves, finely chopped
30 ml/2 tablespoons chopped fresh parsley
salt and freshly ground black pepper

To clean the fresh clams, put them in a sink and scrub them thoroughly with a hard brush, scraping off any barnacles with a knife. Discard any clams which are not tightly closed and put the rest in a colander under cold running water. Leave them for 20 minutes.

When they are clean, place the clams in a large saucepan. Cover and cook over high heat until the clams are open, shaking the pan occasionally. Remove the clam meat from the shells and discard the shells. Strain the liquid left in the pan through a piece of muslin or absorbent kitchen paper and reduce it over high heat. You should have no more than 200 ml/7 fl oz.

Drop the spaghetti into rapidly boiling salted water and cook until *al dente*, firm to the bite.

While the pasta is cooking, heat the oil with the garlic in a frying pan large enough to contain all the pasta. Add the clams (and their strained liquid, if fresh) and cook for 1 minute, stirring constantly. Add the parsley and pepper and taste. Add salt if necessary. Mix well.

When the pasta is ready, drain it and add to the clams in the frying pan. Cook for 1 minute, tossing well.

Spaghettini al Sugo del Settecento
Thin spaghetti with sweet and hot tomato sauce

CAMPANIA

This is an eighteenth century sauce from the recipe book of the Neapolitan Prince of Francavilla. The prince dictated all his recipes to his secretary, who, like his master, was a great gourmet.

Preparation time: 10 minutes (plus 1 hour marinating)
Cooking time: 10 minutes
Serves: 4 as a first course

plain tomato sauce made with 500 g/1 lb tomatoes (see page 132)
75 ml/5 tablespoons olive oil
2 cloves
1 fresh chilli, seeded and finely chopped
5 ml/1 level teaspoon sugar
2·5 ml/½ level teaspoon ground cinnamon
75 g/3 oz freshly grated Parmesan cheese
400 g/14 oz thin spaghetti
salt and freshly ground black pepper

Mix all the ingredients, except the Parmesan, pasta and seasoning, together and leave to marinate for 1 hour.

Ten minutes before serving, drop the spaghetti into rapidly boiling salted water and cook until *al dente*, firm to the bite.

Meanwhile, warm the sauce over very low heat, but do not bring to the boil; then discard the cloves and season to taste.

When the pasta is cooked, drain it, turn it into a serving dish and toss with the sauce and half the Parmesan.

Serve at once, with the remaining Parmesan in a separate bowl.

Spaghetti alla Carbonara *Spaghetti with eggs and bacon*

LAZIO

This sauce is named after the *carbonari*, woodcutters, who used to go up into the Appenine mountains to collect firewood. This nourishing and quickly-made dish used to be their staple diet. Now *Spaghetti alla Carbonara* has become very popular all over Italy.

Preparation time: 10 minutes
Cooking time: 15 minutes
Serves: 4 as a first course

15 ml/1 tablespoon olive or good vegetable
   oil
1 garlic clove
100 g/4 oz lean unsmoked bacon, cut into
   thin strips
400 g/14 oz spaghetti
3 eggs
60 ml/4 tablespoons freshly grated
   Parmesan cheese
30 ml/2 tablespoons single cream
salt and freshly ground black pepper
25 g/1 oz butter

Heat the oil and the whole garlic clove in a large frying pan and add the bacon. Sauté for about 10 minutes, until the bacon is golden brown. Discard the garlic. Drop the spaghetti into rapidly boiling salted water and cook until *al dente*, firm to the bite.

Meanwhile, lightly beat the eggs and combine with the cheese, cream, salt and a generous amount of black pepper. Drain the pasta, return it to the saucepan and toss with the butter, then add it to the bacon in the frying pan. Cook for 1 minute, stirring the whole time. Remove from the heat and pour over the egg and cheese mixture. Mix well and serve at once.

Spaghetti coi Peperoni Arrostiti *Spaghetti with grilled peppers*

BASILICATA

Basilicata, the smallest and poorest of all Italian regions, is blessed only with the scorching sun. This makes peppers grown there very beautiful for their bright colours and very good to eat. This sauce combines the sweetness of the red and yellow peppers with the hotness of the chilli perfectly. You will need to use either a gas flame or a grill to prepare this dish.

Preparation time: 20 minutes
Cooking time: 10 minutes
Serves: 4 as a first course

4 large yellow or red peppers
400 g/14 oz spaghetti
2 garlic cloves, very finely sliced
100 ml/4 fl oz olive oil
2·5-cm/1-inch piece of fresh chilli, seeded
   and very finely chopped
salt
30 ml/2 tablespoons chopped fresh parsley

Place the peppers under a grill or on a wire rack directly over a gas flame. Cook, turning constantly, until the skin is black and charred all over. Peel off the burnt skin with a small sharp knife and then wipe the peppers with absorbent kitchen paper. Cut the grilled peppers into lengthwise strips.

Drop the spaghetti into rapidly boiling salted water and cook until *al dente*, firm to the bite.

While the spaghetti is cooking, put the garlic and the oil in a large frying pan and sauté for 30 seconds. Add the peppers and the chilli and cook gently for 4 minutes, stirring frequently. Add salt to taste.

When the pasta is ready, drain and add it to the frying pan. Sprinkle with the parsley and fry for a further 1 minute, tossing frequently.

Fettuccine alla Panna *Fettuccine with cream*

LAZIO

Also known as *Fettuccine all' Alfredo*, this is a variation of the recipe made famous by Alfredo, a Roman restaurateur. It uses *fettuccine*, the Roman version of *tagliatelle*, which are slightly thicker and narrower.

Preparation time: 5 minutes (plus about 1–1½ hours for pasta making)
Cooking time: 5–8 minutes
Oven temperature: 150°C, 300°F, Gas Mark 2
Serves: 4 as a first course

175 ml/6 fl oz double cream
50 g/2 oz freshly grated Parmesan cheese
pasta made with 3 eggs and 300 g/11 oz flour (see page 139) or 400 g/14 oz bought fettuccine tagliatelle
25 g/1 oz butter
salt and freshly ground black pepper

Put the cream and half the cheese in a large ovenproof serving bowl and place the bowl in the oven for about 5 minutes, while the pasta is cooking.

Meanwhile, drop the pasta into rapidly boiling salted water and cook until *al dente*, firm to the bite.

Drain the pasta and turn it into the bowl containing the cream and cheese. Add the butter and a generous amount of pepper. Toss well. Serve immediately with the remaining Parmesan in a separate bowl.

Conchigliette con Salsa di Gorgonzola, Pistacchio e Cognac *Pasta shells with Gorgonzola, pistachio nuts and brandy*

LOMBARDY

Gorgonzola, not far from the centre of Milan, used to be a village surrounded by green fields. There the Alpine cows used to stop on their way down to the plains in the autumn, and again in the spring as they returned. Thus twice a year Gorgonzola was awash with milk, from which the famous cheese was made. Now, although it is just a suburb of Milan, Gorgonzola is still a great cheese-making centre.

Preparation time: 10 minutes
Cooking time: 15 minutes
Serves: 4 as a first course

30 ml/2 tablespoons shelled pistachio nuts, blanched and skinned
400 g/14 oz small shells or other small tubular pasta
salt and freshly ground black pepper
100 g/4 oz butter
100 g/4 oz Gorgonzola cheese
100 ml/4 fl oz single cream
30 ml/2 tablespoons brandy

Pound the pistachios in a mortar or grind them in a liquidiser or processor. Cook the pasta in rapidly boiling salted water.

While the pasta is cooking, melt the butter and cheese in a double boiler or heavy-based saucepan. Add the cream and cook very gently for 5 minutes, stirring all the time. Remove from the heat and add the pistachios, brandy and a generous amount of black pepper. Taste and add salt if necessary.

Drain the pasta when it is *al dente*, firm to the bite. Turn it into a warm serving dish and pour over the sauce. Mix well and serve at once.

Cozze Ripiene *Stuffed mussels*

PUGLIA

The Italians love stuffed food of every kind. They even manage to stuff mussels, in this case with the local *pecorino* cheese, the well seasoned and piquant kind.

Preparation time: 40 minutes
Cooking time: 10 minutes
Oven temperature: 230°C, 450°F,
   Gas Mark 8
Serves: 6 as a first course

2 litres/2 quarts or 1·25–1·5 kg/2½–3 lb
   mussels in their shells
150 ml/10 level tablespoons fresh dried
   breadcrumbs
150 ml/10 tablespoons chopped fresh parsley
2 garlic cloves, finely chopped
salt and freshly ground black pepper
100 ml/4 fl oz olive oil
25 ml/5 teaspoons freshly grated Parmesan
   cheese

To clean the mussels, put them in a sink and scrub them thoroughly with a hard brush, scraping off any barnacles with a knife. Discard any mussels which are not tightly closed and put the rest in a colander under cold running water. Leave them for about 20 minutes.

When they are clean, place the mussels in a large saucepan. Cover and cook over high heat until the mussels are open, shaking the pan occasionally. Shell the mussels, reserving one half of each empty shell.

Strain the mussel liquid through a sieve lined with absorbent kitchen paper. Mix together the breadcrumbs, parsley, garlic and plenty of pepper. Add the oil and 60 ml/4 tablespoons of the mussel liquid. Blend well together. Taste and adjust the seasonings.

Place the mussels in their shells on 2 baking sheets. With your fingers, pick up a good pinch of the breadcrumb mixture and press it down on each mussel, covering it well and filling the shell. Sprinkle with the Parmesan. Bake in the oven for 10 minutes, moving the baking sheets from top to bottom half way through the cooking.

Serve either hot as an antipasto or cold with French bread.

Cozze Ripiene

Pasta al Tonno *Pasta with tuna fish sauce*

SICILY

This sauce combines two of the favourite and most prevalent fish of Sicily—tuna and anchovy.

Preparation time: 10 minutes
Cooking time: 20 minutes
Serves: 4 as a first course

1 small onion, finely chopped
2 garlic cloves, finely chopped
75 ml/5 tablespoons olive oil
4 anchovy fillets
350 g/12 oz tomatoes, skinned, or 226-g/
   8-oz can plum tomatoes, with their juice
200-g/7-oz can tuna, drained and flaked
salt and freshly ground black pepper
30 ml/2 tablespoons chopped fresh parsley
350 g/12 oz penne or other short tubular
   pasta

In a frying pan, cook the onion and garlic in the oil over low heat until pale golden. Add the anchovy fillets and mash them with a fork. Stir in the tomatoes, roughly chopped, raise the heat to moderate and cook for 5 minutes. Add the tuna, taste and adjust the seasonings. Continue cooking over moderate heat for 20 minutes. Add the parsley.

Meanwhile, drop the pasta into rapidly boiling salted water and cook until *al dente*, firm to the bite. Drain the pasta and turn into a heated dish. Cover with the sauce, toss and serve at once.

Pasta con la Mollica *Pasta with olive oil, breadcrumbs and oregano*

CALABRIA

Although on Christmas Eve no meat is eaten, some of the best dishes in the Italian cuisine are among the food traditionally served on that day. Many of them are based on fish and, like this one, are very simple. Although this may sound a poor way to dress pasta, if you use the best olive oil you will think otherwise. Some cooks add stoned black olives or anchovy fillets to the pasta.

Preparation time: 10 minutes
Cooking time: 15 minutes
Serves: 4 as a first course

400 g/14 oz bucatini or other short tubular
   pasta
100 ml/4 fl oz olive oil
2 garlic cloves, thinly sliced
5 ml/1 teaspoon dried oregano
75 g/3 oz fresh dried breadcrumbs
salt and freshly ground black pepper

Drop the pasta into rapidly boiling salted water and cook until *al dente*, firm to the bite, and drain.

Meanwhile heat 75 ml/3 fl oz of the oil in a large frying pan and add the garlic and oregano. Cook for 30 seconds and then add the breadcrumbs, salt and plenty of black pepper. As soon as the oil has been absorbed add the pasta, pour over the remaining oil and sauté for 2 minutes, stirring frequently. Serve from the pan.

Pasta con le Zucchine *Pasta with courgettes*

VENETO

A good simple recipe which I tasted in Venice and which is well worth trying. It is usually served without cheese, but you can hand around a bowl of grated Parmesan, if you wish.

Preparation time: 25 minutes
Cooking time: 15 minutes
Serves: 4 as a first course

500 g/1 lb courgettes, finely sliced
salt and freshly ground black pepper
1 garlic clove, finely chopped
60 ml/4 tablespoons vegetable oil
25 g/1 oz butter
350 g/12 oz short cut pasta, such as
*   macaroni or penne*
30 ml/2 tablespoons chopped fresh parsley

Put the courgettes in a colander, sprinkle with salt and leave to drain for 20 minutes, then dry thoroughly with absorbent kitchen paper. In a large frying pan, sauté the courgettes and garlic in the oil and butter, for about 10–15 minutes, until soft. Season.

To cook the pasta drop it into a saucepan of rapidly boiling salted water. When *al dente*, firm to the bite, drain well and transfer to the frying pan. Sprinkle with the parsley and toss in the sauce for 1 minute over heat. Serve at once.

Mozzarella in Carrozza *Fried mozzarella sandwiches*

CAMPANIA

The Italian name of this popular dish literally means '*mozzarella* in a carriage'. It is, in fact, a very grand name for a cheap dish, since *mozzarella* costs very little in Campania. If you cannot find Italian *mozzarella*, use *Bel Paese*.

Preparation and cooking time: 30 minutes
Serves: 4

200 g/7 oz mozzarella, cut into 0·5-cm/
*   ¼-inch slices*
8 large slices of white bread, crustless and
*   cut in half*
salt and freshly ground black pepper
225 ml/8 fl oz milk
2 eggs
75 g/3 oz flour
vegetable oil

Divide the mozzarella into 8 equal portions. Lay each portion on a half-slice of bread, sprinkle with salt and pepper and cover with another piece of bread.

Pour the milk into a soup plate. In another soup plate beat the eggs together with a little salt and pepper. Spread the flour on a board or a plate. Very quickly dip each sandwich into the milk, coat lightly with the flour and then dip it into the eggs, letting any excess egg flow back into the plate.

Meanwhile pour enough oil into a frying pan to come 1 cm/½ inch up the side of the pan and heat it quickly. When the oil is very hot, but not smoking, slip the sandwiches carefully into the pan in a single layer. Fry them until they are a deep golden brown on each side. Drain on absorbent kitchen paper and serve.

Pasta con Salsa di Funghi e Panna

Pasta con Salsa di Funghi e Panna Pasta with mushroom and cream sauce

VENEZIA-TRIDENTINA, VENETO

In Trento on the Adige River, this dish is made with wild mushrooms, which are easily obtainable in Italian shops during the mushroom season, or freshly picked in the countryside. I find that cultivated mushrooms do not have enough flavour for this recipe, so I always add some dried wild mushrooms.

Preparation time: 15 minutes
Cooking time: 10 minutes
Serves: 4 as a first course

10-g/⅓ oz packet dried boletus funghi
40 g/1½ oz butter
15 ml/1 tablespoon vegetable oil
1 garlic clove, slightly crushed
30 ml/2 tablespoons chopped fresh parsley
100 g/4 oz mushrooms, roughly chopped
salt and freshly ground black pepper
30 ml/2 fl oz double cream
400 g/14 oz spaghetti or fusilli
freshly grated Parmesan cheese

Soak the dried mushrooms in a cupful of warm water for 20 minutes, then lift them out with a slotted spoon and roughly chop them. Strain the mushroom liquid into a bowl, through a sieve lined with absorbent kitchen paper, and reserve.

Melt the butter and oil in a large frying pan and add the whole garlic clove and parsley. Cook for 1 minute, stirring constantly. Add the dried mushrooms and about 75 ml/3 fl oz of the reserved mushroom liquid and simmer for 5 minutes. Discard the garlic clove, add the cultivated mushrooms and seasonings and cook for 2 to 3 minutes, stirring frequently. As soon as the mushrooms have released their juice, turn the heat up to high and cook for a further 3 minutes. Remove from the heat and add the cream, toss well and adjust seasonings.

Meanwhile drop the pasta into rapidly boiling salted water and cook until *al dente*, firm to the bite. Drain and turn into the frying pan. Toss with the sauce for 1 minute over heat and serve at once with a bowl of grated Parmesan.

Orecchiette con i Broccoli *Pasta with broccoli*

PUGLIA

Orecchiette, meaning 'little ears', is a kind of home-made pasta made from durum wheat flour and water. It is difficult to make but commercially-made pasta, such as penne, makes an excellent substitute. Occasionally you can find *orecchiette* in an Italian shop.

This recipe uses the broccoli florets only. Do not discard the stems and leaves as they are delicious boiled and dressed with lemon juice and oil.

Preparation time: 20 minutes
Cooking time: 15 minutes
Serves: 4 as a first course

500 g/1 lb broccoli, with fairly large florets
45 ml/3 level tablespoons sultanas
1 small onion, sliced into rings
90 ml/6 tablespoons olive oil
4 anchovy fillets
25 g/1 oz pine nuts
salt and freshly ground black pepper
400 g/14 oz penne, macaroni or large cut
  tubular pasta
25 g/1 oz butter
50 g/2 oz freshly grated Romano or
  Parmesan cheese

Wash the broccoli and separate the florets from the stems and leaves. Drop the florets into a saucepan of boiling salted water and cook for 5 to 7 minutes, until tender. Drain well and set aside.

Soak the sultanas in a cupful of warm water. Sauté the onion in 60 ml/4 tablespoons of the oil until soft and golden, but not brown. While the onion is cooking, heat the remaining oil in a small pan. Remove from the heat, add the anchovy fillets and mash with a fork.

Add the broccoli and the anchovy paste to the onion and stir gently over low heat. Drain the sultanas and add to the broccoli sauce with the pine nuts. Season with pepper, taste and add salt if necessary.

Meanwhile, drop the pasta into rapidly boiling salted water and cook until it is *al dente*, firm to the bite; drain it and turn into a warm serving dish. Toss with the butter and the cheese. Pour over the broccoli sauce and serve at once.

Orecchiette con i Broccoli

Maccheroncini all'Insalata   *Macaroni with anchovy fillets and grilled peppers*

BASILICATA

This is not a traditional way of serving pasta and, indeed, the thought of eating cold pasta would horrify many Italians. However, I feel that this modern invention must now have a place in a book of Italian cooking. The pasta should be served tepid rather than cold, or else it will become too gluey. You can make your own variations using your favourite salad dressings.

Preparation time: 15 minutes (plus 1 hour cooling)
Cooking time: 10 minutes
Serves: 4 as a first course

1 red or yellow pepper
225 g/8 oz tomatoes, skinned, seeded and
   cut into thin strips
6 anchovy fillets, pounded to a paste
1 garlic clove, crushed
1-cm/½-inch piece of fresh chilli, seeded and
   very finely chopped
75 ml/5 tablespoons olive oil
350 g/12 oz small macaroni
30 ml/2 tablespoons chopped fresh parsley

Place the pepper under a preheated grill or on a wire rack directly over a gas flame. Cook, turning, until the skin is black and charred all over. Peel off the burnt skin, using a small knife. Wipe the pepper with absorbent kitchen paper, then cut into quarters; remove and discard the seeds and white ribs and cut into thin strips.

In a salad bowl, mix together the strips of pepper and tomato, with the anchovy paste, garlic, chilli and oil.

Cook the pasta in boiling salted water until *al dente*, firm to the bite. Drain and turn into the bowl. Toss well, check seasoning and allow to cool for about 1 hour.

Just before serving sprinkle with parsley.

Bucatini all'Amatriciana   *Bucatini with salt pork*

LAZIO

This is one of the most popular sauces for pasta. You will find it on the menu of many restaurants all over Italy and even in this country. In Lazio and Abruzzi it is usually made with pork jowl.

Preparation time: 10 minutes
Cooking time: 30 minutes
Serves: 4

45 ml/3 tablespoons olive oil
225 g/8 oz salt pork, or lean unsmoked
   bacon, cut into matchsticks
225 g/8 oz tomatoes, skinned and roughly
   chopped, or 226-g/8-oz can plum
   tomatoes, with their juice
½ small onion, finely chopped
2·5-cm/1-inch piece of fresh chilli, seeded
   and finely chopped
salt
350 g/12 oz bucatini
50 g/2 oz freshly grated Romano or
   Parmesan cheese

Heat the oil in a saucepan, add the pork and sauté for 10 minutes, stirring frequently. Remove the meat from the pan with a slotted spoon and set aside.

Add the tomatoes and the onion to the saucepan and cook for 5 minutes until soft. Return the meat to the pan and add the chilli and cook, over low heat, for a further 15 minutes until tender. Remove the chilli. Taste and adjust the seasonings. You might not need to add any salt, because of the saltiness of the pork.

While the sauce is cooking, drop the pasta into rapidly boiling salted water and cook until *al dente*, firm to the bite.

Drain and turn it into a heated bowl, cover with the sauce, sprinkle with the cheese, toss well and serve at once.

SOUPS

Minestrone   *Vegetable, bean and rice soup*

The famous *minestrone* is made differently all over Italy. In the north rice is usually included, in central Italy it is made with pasta and in the south with vegetables only. This recipe is for *Minestrone alla Milanese*, which is claimed to be the original one. It is served hot in winter and at room temperature in summer. It tastes even better if made a day in advance.

*Preparation time: 40 minutes (plus 8 hours
for soaking the beans)*
Cooking time: 2½ hours
Serves: 8

50 g/2 oz butter
50 g/2 oz pancetta or unsmoked streaky
   bacon
3 onions, sliced
1 garlic clove, chopped
2 carrots, diced
2 celery sticks, diced
350 g/12 oz potatoes, diced
225 g/8 oz dried borlotti beans, soaked in
   cold water overnight or 397-g/14-oz can
   cannellini beans, drained
2 courgettes, diced
100 g/4 oz shelled fresh or frozen peas
225 g/8 oz cabbage, preferably Savoy,
   shredded
2·4 litres/4 pints meat stock (see page 138)
225 g/8 oz tomatoes, skinned and roughly
   chopped, or 226-g/8-oz can tomatoes,
   with their juice
salt and freshly ground black pepper
15 ml/1 tablespoon chopped fresh parsley
175 g/6 oz arborio or long-grain rice
40 g/1½ oz freshly grated Parmesan cheese

Choose a saucepan large enough to hold all the ingredients and in it heat the butter and sauté the pancetta, onions and garlic for about 5 minutes, until soft. Add the carrots and celery, and sauté for 2 minutes. Put in the potatoes and the dried beans (if used) and stir. After a further 2 minutes, add the courgettes and the peas, and, lastly, after a few more minutes, the cabbage, stirring well after each addition. Cover with the stock, add the tomatoes and the parsley.

Bring to the boil then simmer for about 2 hours, until the beans are tender. Add the rice, stir and then add the canned beans (if used). Cook for about 15 minutes (less for long-grain rice), until the rice is *al dente*, firm to the bite. Remove from the heat, add the Parmesan, salt and pepper, taste and adjust the seasonings.

Serve piping hot.

Pasta e Fagioli all'Ischitiana   *Pasta and dried bean soup*

CAMPANIA

Bean soup is made in many regions of Italy, sometimes with the addition of pasta or rice. There are also variations in the type of fat in which it is cooked. The Venetians, for example, use a ham bone to give added flavour and nourishment.

This version, from the island of Ischia in the gulf of Naples, is one of the lightest, if a bean soup could ever be called light. The pasta used is called *munnezzaglia*, a mixture of the different shapes left at the bottom of used pasta packets.

I always make this soup a day in advance because I find its flavour really improves.

Preparation time: 10 minutes (plus
  overnight soaking)
Cooking time: 2½ hours
Serves: 4

175 g/6 oz dried cannellini or haricot beans,
  soaked overnight
1 garlic clove, roughly chopped
1 celery stick, chopped
500 g/1 lb tomatoes, skinned and chopped or
  397-g/14-oz can plum tomatoes, with
  their juice
1-cm/½-inch piece of fresh chilli, seeded and
  finely chopped
100 ml/4 fl oz olive oil
4–5 basil leaves, if available or 15 ml/1
  tablespoon chopped fresh parsley
100 g/4 oz ditalini or a mixture of any short
  pasta
salt and freshly ground black pepper

Rinse and drain the beans. Place the beans, the garlic, celery, tomatoes and chilli in a large saucepan. Cover with 1·7 litres/3 pints of cold water. Do not add salt at this stage or the beans will not become tender. Bring slowly to the boil and cook, covered, over a very low heat for about 2 hours until the beans are tender.

Add the oil, basil or parsley, the pasta and salt and pepper to taste. Stir well and return the soup to the boil. Cover and simmer for about 15 minutes, until the pasta is *al dente*, firm to the bite. The soup can be served either hot or at room temperature.

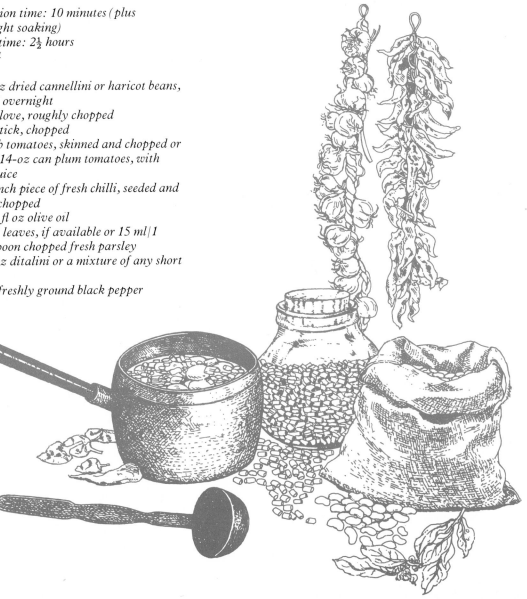

Minestra coi Pomodori *Pasta and tomato soup*

CALABRIA

Very simply made from the best ingredients, *Minestra coi Pomodori* was often the Italian peasant's main dish. This recipe comes from the foot of Italy, but variations of it are made all over the country.

Preparation time: 10 minutes
Cooking time: 30 minutes
Serves: 6

75 ml/3 fl oz olive oil
2 garlic cloves, lightly crushed
5 tomatoes, skinned and coarsely chopped
2 onions, thinly sliced
45 ml/3 tablespoons chopped fresh parsley
salt and freshly ground black pepper
150 g/5 oz ditalini or any other small short cut pasta
30 ml/2 tablespoons freshly grated Parmesan cheese

Heat the oil in a large saucepan and sauté the whole garlic cloves until just coloured. Discard the garlic. Add the tomatoes, onions and half the chopped parsley and fry gently for 10 minutes, stirring frequently. Pour over 1·5 litres/2½ pints of water and add salt and plenty of pepper. Simmer, covered, for 20 minutes. Raise the heat and drop in the pasta. Stir well with a wooden spoon. Cook over moderate heat for about 10 minutes until the pasta is *al dente*, firm to the bite.

Just before serving, add the remaining parsley and the Parmesan cheese. Mix well and serve.

Cipollata *Onion and tomato soup*

UMBRIA

A really filling peasant soup from central Italy, which is perfect for a cold winter night. The inclusion of basil gives *Cipollata* a subtle flavour and aroma.

Preparation time: 20 minutes
Cooking time: 1½ hours
Serves: 4

50 g/2 oz pancetta or unsmoked streaky bacon
30 ml/2 tablespoons olive oil
800 g/1¾ lb onions, very finely sliced
1 litre/1¾ pints chicken stock or 2 chicken stock cubes dissolved in the same quantity of water
396-g/14-oz can plum tomatoes, with their juice
1-cm/½-inch piece of fresh chilli, seeded and finely chopped
salt and freshly ground black pepper
6–7 fresh basil leaves, torn or 10 ml/2 teaspoons dried basil
45 ml/3 tablespoons freshly grated Romano or Parmesan cheese
8 slices of stale French bread, toasted
1 garlic clove

In a large saucepan, fry the pancetta or bacon in the oil for 2 to 3 minutes until soft. Add the onions, cover the pan and cook very gently for about 1 hour, until the onions are reduced to a paste. Add the stock, tomatoes, chilli and salt and pepper. Cover and cook for a further 30 minutes. Just before serving, add the basil and the grated cheese and adjust the seasonings.

Rub the toasted bread with the garlic clove. Put 2 slices in each soup plate and pour over the soup to serve.

Zuppa di Zucchine *Courgette soup*

BASILICATA

A lovely looking soup—pale green speckled with yellow, *Zuppa di Zucchine* combines colour with flavour. The eggs added at the end of the cooking should curdle and thicken the broth. For this soup I strongly recommend using home-made stock (see page 138).

Preparation time: 25–35 minutes
Cooking time: 35–40 minutes
Serves: 4

300 g/11 oz courgettes, cut into 1-cm/½-inch
  cubes
salt and freshly ground black pepper
1 small onion, chopped
25 g/1 oz butter
30 ml/2 tablespoons vegetable oil
1 litre/1¾ pints beef or chicken stock
2 egg yolks
45 ml/3 tablespoons freshly grated
  Parmesan cheese
pinch of grated nutmeg
30 ml/2 tablespoons single cream

Place the courgettes in a colander, sprinkle with salt and leave to drain for 20 to 30 minutes. Dry them thoroughly with absorbent kitchen paper.

Put the onion, butter and oil in a large saucepan and cook gently until the onion is translucent, but not brown. Add the courgettes and cook for 2 to 3 minutes, stirring all the time. Pour in the stock and simmer, covered, for 30 minutes.

Beat together the yolks, cheese, nutmeg, cream and seasonings. Pour this mixture into the soup, stir well and boil for 1 minute.

Serve at once.

Stracciatella *Broth with eggs*

MARCHE

This excellent soup is made all over central Italy, but it is the Roman version which is most famous and the one usually served in restaurants in Britain. I have chosen a lesser-known recipe, from Marche, in which a little grated lemon rind flavours the broth, instead of the nutmeg used in Rome. Home-made stock is essential for this soup.

Preparation time: 5 minutes
Cooking time: 3 minutes
Serves: 4

1 litre/1¾ pints home-made meat stock (see
  page 138)
3 eggs
45 ml/3 tablespoons freshly grated
  Parmesan cheese
30 ml/2 level tablespoons fresh dried
  breadcrumbs
1·25 ml/¼ level teaspoon grated lemon rind
salt

Heat the stock to simmering point. Beat the eggs in a bowl and add the Parmesan, breadcrumbs, lemon rind and salt. Pour in 1 ladleful of the hot stock. Blend until smooth then pour the mixture slowly into the saucepan of hot stock, beating all the time with a fork. Continue beating the soup over a very low heat, for 3 minutes.

Serve in warm bowls, with crusty bread.

La Minestra di Orazio *Horace's chick-pea and pasta soup*

LAZIO

This recipe is an adaptation of the famous soup eaten in Ancient Rome and referred to by Horace in one of his satires: 'I am going home to a bowl of leeks and chick-peas and lasagne.' This is, in fact, one of the earliest literary references to any kind of pasta.

Preparation time: 10 minutes (plus overnight soaking)
Cooking time: 3¼ hours
Serves: 6

175 g/6 oz dried chick-peas, soaked overnight
1 celery stick, finely chopped
1 leek, white part only, cut into rounds
3–4 tomatoes, skinned, seeded and roughly chopped
1 bay leaf, crumbled
salt and freshly ground black pepper
175 g/6 oz ditalini or any other small tubular pasta
100 ml/4 fl oz olive oil
15 ml/1 tablespoon chopped fresh parsley
freshly grated Parmesan cheese

Drain the chick-peas and rinse with fresh water. Put them in a large saucepan together with the celery, leek, tomatoes and bay leaf and pour over 1·5 litres/2½ pints of water. Cover tightly and bring the soup rapidly to the boil. Lower the heat and simmer for about 3 hours until tender. When cooked, add salt to taste.

Drop the pasta into rapidly boiling salted water and cook for only 10 minutes after the water has returned to the boil. Drain the pasta.

Meanwhile heat the olive oil in a large frying pan. Turn the pasta into the pan, toss in the hot oil for 1 minute and then pour the pasta and oil into the soup. Cook, uncovered, until the pasta is *al dente*, firm to the bite. This should only take a minute or two.

Adjust the seasoning, discard the bay leaf, sprinkle with the parsley and serve with a bowl of Parmesan.

Zuppa di Fave *Broad bean soup*

TUSCANY

The broad beans from central Italy are the best in the world. They are so tiny and sweet that, in Tuscany particularly, they are often eaten raw with local cheese, such as *pecorino*. The piquancy of a well-seasoned *pecorino* is slightly mellowed by the sweetness of young beans. For this soup the beans should be skinned, unless they are young and freshly picked.

Preparation time: 45 minutes
Cooking time: 15 minutes
Serves: 4

45 ml/3 tablespoons olive oil
1 large onion, cut into rings
1 garlic clove, sliced
1·25 kg/2½ lb broad beans, shelled
30 ml/2 level tablespoons tomato purée
1·5 litres/2½ pints home-made meat stock (see page 138)
1 bay leaf
salt and freshly ground black pepper
30 ml/2 level tablespoons ricotta cheese

Heat the oil in a saucepan and add the onion and the garlic. Sauté until golden. Add the beans and the tomato purée and fry gently for 30 seconds, stirring all the time. Pour in the stock, add the bay leaf, stir and cook, covered, for about 10 minutes, until the beans are cooked. Taste and add salt and pepper. Discard the bay leaf and sieve the soup. Lift the broad beans out of the sieve with a spoon and peel them as soon as they are cool enough to handle. Lift the onion rings out of the sieve and set them aside with the peeled beans.

Return the soup to the saucepan. Add the peeled beans and the onion rings. Bring the soup to the boil, add the ricotta, stir well and boil for 1 minute. Serve immediately.

Ciuppin *Creamed fish soup*

LIGURIA

This is similar to *Bouillabaisse*, but more elegant and much easier to eat because the fish is puréed after cooking. However it does require a longer preparation in the kitchen. Don't leave out the fish heads—they give the soup a delicious flavour.

Preparation time: 40 minutes
Cooking time: 40 minutes
Serves: 8

1 kg/2 lb assorted fish, such as red mullet,
*   grouper, dogfish, roach, whiting, John*
*   Dory*
1 large onion, sliced
1 celery stick, trimmed and chopped
1 carrot, chopped
1 garlic clove, chopped
100 ml/4 fl oz olive oil
150 ml/¼ pint dry white wine
226-g/8-oz can plum tomatoes, with their
*   juice*
salt and freshly ground black pepper
45 ml/3 tablespoons chopped fresh parsley

Clean and wash the fish and cut into large chunks, leaving the heads on.

In a large saucepan, fry all the vegetables and the garlic gently in 75 ml/3 fl oz of the oil for 10 minutes, stirring frequently. Pour over the wine and boil rapidly to reduce by half. Add the fish, mix thoroughly and fry gently for 10 minutes, turning it over occasionally.

Pour over 2 litres/3½ pints of boiling water, add the tomatoes and the seasoning, return the soup to the boil and simmer, covered, for 30 minutes.

Leave the soup aside to cool and then lift the fish out on to a plate. Remove the heads, the backbones and the fins and discard. Strain the stock, reserving the vegetables. Purée the fish and the vegetables through the coarsest holes of a food-mill into a clean saucepan and cover with the reserved stock.

Reheat the soup and just before serving, adjust the seasoning, and add the remaining oil and the parsley. Serve with croûtons.

Zuppa alla Pavese *Soup with eggs and cheese*

LOMBARDY

Pavia, a provincial town south-west of Milan which was a great mediaeval trading centre, is nowadays famous for two things: the Certosa, a magnificent Carthusian monastery, and the nourishing *Zuppa alla Pavese*.

This soup is a meal in its own right, quickly prepared and very warming. One essential factor is that it must be made with home-made stock. If you are lucky enough to live in the country and can get very fresh eggs, the result is even better.

Preparation time: 5 minutes
Cooking time: 5 minutes
Serves: 4

1 litre/1¾ pints home-made stock
*   (see page 138)*
50 g/2 oz butter
4 slices white bread
60 ml/4 tablespoons freshly grated
*   Parmesan cheese*
4 eggs
salt and freshly ground black pepper

Heat the stock until simmering.

Meanwhile melt the butter in a frying pan. When it is very hot, but not burnt, add the bread slices and fry on both sides until golden.

Place one slice of the fried bread in each of four warmed soup bowls, sprinkle with 7·5 ml/½ tablespoon of Parmesan and gently break an egg on to the bread. Season with a little salt and plenty of black pepper and sprinkle with the remaining cheese.

Pour over the simmering stock very slowly, being careful not to break the egg yolk. Serve at once.

If you prefer eggs well cooked poach them in the stock before lifting them on to the bread in the soup bowl.

PASTA, PIZZA
AND
OMELETTES

Lasagne Verdi al Forno *Baked green lasagne*

EMILIA-ROMAGNA

The baked *lasagne* often served in restaurants here in England is a far cry from the real thing you eat in Bologna, where the dish is richly laced rather than smothered with sauce.

Preparation time: 15 minutes (plus about
*   1 hour for pasta making)*
Cooking time: 2 hours minimum for the
*   bolognese sauce plus 15 minutes for baking*
Oven temperature: 220°C, 425°F,
*   Gas Mark 7*
Serves: 4 as a main course, 6 as a first course

lasagne verde made with 2 eggs and
*   250 g/9 oz plain flour (see page 139) or*
*   350 g/12 oz bought lasagne verde*
bolognese sauce (see recipe on page 130)
béchamel sauce made with 750 ml/1¼ pints
*   milk, 75 g/3 oz butter and 65 g/2½ oz flour*
*   (see page 133)*
75 g/3 oz freshly grated Parmesan cheese
15 g/½ oz butter

Make the pasta as directed on page 139. To cook the home-made pasta, bring a large saucepan of salted water to the boil. Place a large bowl of cold water near the cooker and lay some clean dry kitchen cloths nearby. When the water boils, drop in 5 or 6 rectangles of pasta and stir with a wooden spoon. Cook for 20 seconds after the water has come back to the boil, then lift each sheet of pasta out with a fish slice and plunge it into the bowl of cold water. Lift it out and lay it on the cloths. Repeat this operation until all the pasta is cooked. Pat the top of the lasagne dry.

If you are using bought lasagne, cook according to the directions on the packet.

Butter a 30 × 20-cm/12 × 8-inch ovenproof dish generously. Spread 30 ml/2 tablespoons of the bolognese sauce on the bottom, cover with a layer of lasagne and spread over a little bolognese sauce and some béchamel. Sprinkle with grated cheese. Cover with another layer of lasagne and repeat until all ingredients are used, finishing with a layer of béchamel. Sprinkle with the remaining cheese and dot with a little butter.

Bake in the oven for 15 to 20 minutes until the top has formed a golden crust. Allow the dish to settle for at least 5 minutes before serving.

Timpano di Lasagne alla Montefeltro
Baked lasagne with prosciutto and cheese

MARCHE

This *pasticcio* (see page 44) was served as an entrée at the court of the Duke of Montefeltro at his palace in Urbino during the fifteenth century.

Preparation time: 20 minutes (plus 1–1½
*   hours for pasta making)*
Cooking time: 30 minutes
Oven temperature: 200°C, 400°F,
*   Gas Mark 6*
Serves: 4 as a main course

lasagne made with 4 eggs, 400 g/14 oz flour
*   (see page 139), or 500 g/1 lb bought*
*   lasagne*
15 ml/1 tablespoon vegetable oil
150 ml/¼ pint double cream
50 g/2 oz mozzarella cheese, diced
50 g/2 oz Bel Paese cheese, diced
salt and freshly ground black pepper
115 g/4½ oz prosciutto, cut into thin strips
50 g/2 oz butter
100 g/4 oz freshly grated Parmesan cheese
béchamel sauce made with 568 ml/
*   1 pint milk, 65 g/2½ oz butter and*
*   50 g/2 oz flour (see page 133), and*
*   flavoured with 1·25 ml/¼ teaspoon grated*
*   nutmeg*

Make the pasta as directed on page 139. To cook the home-made pasta, bring a large saucepan of salted water to the boil with the vegetable oil. Place a large bowl of cold water near the cooker and lay some clean dry kitchen towels nearby. When the water boils, drop in 5 or 6 sheets of pasta and stir with a wooden spoon. Cook for 20 seconds after the water has come back to the boil then lift each pasta sheet out with a fish slice and plunge it into the bowl of cold water. Lift out and lay on the tea towels to dry. Repeat this operation until all the pasta has been cooked. Gently pat the lasagne dry.

If you are using bought lasagne, cook according to the directions on the packet.

Butter a large deep ovenproof dish and pour in 30 ml/2 tablespoons of the cream. Mix together the diced cheeses with the remaining cream. Add pepper, taste and add salt if necessary. Fill the dish with alternative layers of lasagne and the cheese and cream mixture, sprinkling the ham over the cheeses. Dot each layer with butter and sprinkle with Parmesan. Finish with a layer of lasagne. Cover the top with the béchamel sauce.

Bake in the oven for about 20 minutes, until golden brown.

Allow to settle for 5 minutes before serving.

Lasagne Verdi al Forno

Pasticcio di Lasagne alla Rossini

Lasagne with meatballs, cheese and béchamel sauce

MARCHE

Rossini may not qualify as one of the greatest composers but he would certainly have been a contender for the greatest musical gourmet. This *pasticcio* is supposed to have been created by the maestro himself.

*Preparation time: 30 minutes (plus about
    1–1½ hours for pasta making)*
Cooking time: 20 minutes
*Oven temperature: 200°C, 400°F,
    Gas Mark 6*
*Serves: 4 as a main course, 6 as a first
    course*

350 g/12 oz minced beef
1 egg
¼ garlic clove, finely chopped
30 ml/2 tablespoons freshly grated
    Parmesan cheese
flour
salt and freshly ground black pepper
60 ml/4 tablespoons vegetable oil
60 ml/4 tablespoons dry white wine
béchamel sauce (see page 133) made with
    750 ml/1¼ pints milk, 60 g/2½ oz flour
    and 75 g/3 oz butter
pinch of grated nutmeg
100 g/4 oz mild cured ham, chopped
100 g/4 oz mozzarella or Bel Paese cheese,
    thinly sliced
150 ml/¼ pint single cream
lasagne, made with 3 eggs, 300 g/11 oz flour
    (see page 139) or 400 g/14 oz bought
    lasagne
15 ml/1 tablespoon vegetable oil
225 ml/8 fl oz plain tomato sauce
    (see page 132)
25 g/1 oz butter

In a bowl, combine the beef, egg, garlic, and 15 ml/1 tablespoon of the Parmesan cheese. Mix well and shape the mixture into small balls, each the size of a marble. There should be about 16 balls. Roll them lightly in a little flour seasoned with salt and pepper.

Heat the oil and when it is hot add the meat balls and fry them for about 5 minutes, until they are brown on all sides. Add the wine, increase the heat and cook until the liquid has reduced by half. Drain the meat balls on a piece of absorbent kitchen paper and set aside. Discard the liquid.

Make the béchamel sauce according to the method on page 133. When it is cooked remove from the heat and stir in the nutmeg, ham, sliced cheese and cream.

Make the pasta as directed on page 139. To cook the home-made pasta, bring a large saucepan of salted water containing the vegetable oil to the boil. Place a large bowl of cold water near the cooker and lay some clean dry kitchen cloths nearby. When the water boils, drop in 5 or 6 rectangles of pasta and stir with a wooden spoon. Cook for 20 seconds after the water has come back to the boil and then lift each sheet of pasta out with a fish slice and plunge it into the bowl of cold water. Lift it out and lay it on the cloths. Repeat this operation until all the pasta is cooked. Pat the top of the lasagne dry.

If you are using bought lasagne, cook according to the directions on the packet.

Cover the bottom of a greased 30 × 20-cm/12 × 8-inch ovenproof dish with a layer of lasagne. Do not overlap the pieces by more than 0·5 cm/¼ inch. Distribute a few meat balls over the pasta, and cover with 45 ml/3 tablespoons of tomato sauce and about one quarter of the béchamel sauce. Continue making layers in this way, making sure that the meat balls are evenly distributed through the whole dish. You should have between 4 and 5 layers, finishing with a layer of lasagne topped with béchamel sauce. Sprinkle over the remaining tablespoon of Parmesan cheese, and dot with butter.

Bake in the oven for 15 to 20 minutes, until the top forms a light golden crust. Leave the pasticcio to settle for 5 minutes before serving.

Pasticci

A *pasticcio* is usually made with home-made pasta, such as *lasagne* or *tagliatelle*, or bought *macaroni* or *penne*, and other ingredients such as cheese, vegetables and sauces. All the ingredients are prepared or cooked separately and then combined for a final baking. *Pasticci* were frequently served at banquets during the Renaissance, when they were called *timballi* or *timpani*. Nowadays the word *timballo* is used for dishes which can be turned out of the dish in which they have been baked.

Substantial and nourishing dishes, *pasticci* can be prepared in advance and even frozen although I cannot recommend freezing pasta, as it would lose its fresh taste.

Pasticcio di Lasagne alla Saint-Martin

Baked lasagne with mushrooms and cheeses

VALLE D'AOSTA, PIEDMONT

A recipe that comes from Valle d'Aosta where mushrooms are plentiful in the woods and the local cheeses are rich and sweet. Here I substitute more common cheeses for the original ones, which are not available in this country.

Preparation time: 30 minutes (plus about
  1–1½ hours for pasta making)
Cooking time: 20 minutes
Oven temperature: 200°C, 400°F,
  Gas Mark 6
Serves: 4 as a main course, 6 as a first
  course

500 g/1 lb mushrooms, thinly sliced
1 garlic clove
50 g/2 oz butter
salt and freshly ground black pepper
lasagne made with 3 eggs and 300 g/11 oz
  flour (see page 139) or 400 g/14 oz bought
  lasagne
15 ml/1 tablespoon vegetable oil
150 g/5 oz Bel Paese cheese, cut into very
  thin slices
150 g/5 oz Gruyère cheese, cut into very
  thin slices
75 g/3 oz freshly grated Parmesan cheese
200 ml/7 fl oz double cream

In a frying pan, sauté the mushrooms with the whole garlic clove in 25 g/1 oz of the butter over a high heat. When the mushrooms have absorbed all the butter, add salt and pepper and lower the heat. Cook until the mushrooms have released their liquid and then turn the heat up to high again and cook for 3 minutes. Discard the garlic.

Make the pasta as directed on page 139. To cook the home-made pasta, bring a large saucepan of salted water with the vegetable oil to the boil. Place a large bowl of cold water near the cooker and lay some clean dry kitchen cloths nearby. When the water boils, drop in 5 or 6 rectangles of pasta and stir with a wooden spoon. Cook.for 20 seconds after the water has come back to the boil, then lift each sheet of pasta out with a fish slice and plunge it into the bowl of cold water. Lift it out and lay it on the cloths. Repeat this operation until all the pasta is cooked. Pat the top of the lasagne dry.

If you are using bought lasagne, cook according to the directions on the packet.

Butter a 30 × 23-cm/12 × 9-inch ovenproof dish and cover the bottom with one layer of lasagne. Distribute about a quarter of the mushrooms and of the sliced cheeses evenly over the lasagne layer, sprinkle with 15 ml/1 tablespoon of Parmesan and dot with a little butter. Add another layer of pasta and cover with mushrooms and cheese as before. Repeat until you have used all the ingredients, finishing with a layer of the sliced cheeses. The lasagne should not be too thick: do not make more than 5 to 6 layers of pasta.

Pour over the cream, sprinkle with salt and pepper and the remaining Parmesan and butter. Cover with foil and bake for 10 minutes. Bake uncovered for a further 10 minutes, or until a light crust has formed on the top. Allow to settle for 5 minutes before serving.

Penne ai Quattro Formaggi   *Pasta with four cheeses*

VALLE D'AOSTA, PIEDMONT

Preparation time: 10 minutes
Cooking time: 10–15 minutes
Oven temperature: 200°C, 400°F,
  Gas Mark 6
Serves: 4 as a main course

400 g/14 oz penne or other tubular cut pasta
75 g/3 oz butter, melted
50 g/2 oz freshly grated Parmesan cheese
75 g/3 oz Gruyère cheese, cut into
  matchsticks
75 g/3 oz Bel Paese cheese, cut into
  matchsticks
100 g/4 oz mozzarella cheese, cut into
  matchsticks
salt and freshly ground black pepper

Drop the pasta into rapidly boiling salted water and cook for 10 minutes until *al dente*, firm to the bite. Drain the pasta, return it to the saucepan and toss with half of the butter, and half of the Parmesan. Add the other cheeses and plenty of black pepper and mix thoroughly.

Transfer the pasta mixture to a buttered ovenproof dish. Flatten the top and pour over the remaining butter. Sprinkle with the remaining Parmesan. Bake in the oven for 10 to 15 minutes until the top is crusty and golden. Allow to settle for 5 minutes before serving.

Cannelloni Ripieni di Stracotto *Cannelloni stuffed with braised beef*

Cannelloni can be stuffed with the filling used for *Tortellini* (see page 55) or for *Crespelle alla Fiorentina* (see page 96). This recipe is from Piedmont, whence *Cannelloni* originates—one of the two stuffed pasta which do not come from Emilia-Romagna, the other being ravioli which originated in Liguria.

Preparation time: 30 minutes (plus about
*   1–1½ hours for pasta making)*
Cooking time: 3 hours
Oven temperature: 200°C, 400°F,
*   Gas Mark 6*
Serves: 4 as a main course

50 g/2 oz butter
30 ml/2 tablespoons vegetable oil
1 small onion, very finely chopped
1 small carrot, very finely chopped
1 celery stick, very finely chopped
350 g/12 oz braising steak in one piece
100 ml/4 fl oz red wine
15 ml/1 tablespoon tomato purée diluted in
*   100 ml/4 fl oz meat stock (see page 138)*
salt and freshly ground black pepper
50 g/2 oz fresh dried breadcrumbs
50 g/2 oz freshly grated Parmesan cheese
2 eggs
pinch of grated nutmeg
lasagne made with 3 eggs and 300 g/11 oz
*   flour (see page 139) or 400 g/14 oz*
*   bought lasagne*
15 ml/1 tablespoon vegetable oil
béchamel sauce made with 750 ml/1¼ pints
*   milk, 75 g/3 oz butter and 60 g/2½ oz*
*   flour (see page 133)*

Put 25 g/1 oz of the butter, together with the oil, onion, carrot and celery, in a small saucepan and fry gently for 5 minutes, stirring frequently. Add the meat, raise the heat and brown well on all sides. Pour over the wine and boil rapidly until it has nearly all evaporated. Add the diluted tomato purée, salt and pepper and bring to the boil. Simmer very gently, covered, for 2 to 2½ hours until the meat is tender and the liquid quite thick. Baste frequently and add a little more warm stock or water, if necessary, during the cooking.

Lift the meat from the pot and mince or chop it very finely, but not with a blender or a food processor, which would reduce it to a paste. Transfer the meat with half the cooking liquid to a bowl and set aside.

Put the breadcrumbs and 30 ml/2 level tablespoons Parmesan in a bowl and soak with half the cooking juice of the meat for 10 minutes.

Add the breadcrumbs mixture, the eggs and the nutmeg to the meat in the bowl, and mix very thoroughly. Taste and adjust the seasonings.

Make the pasta as directed on page 139. To cook the home-made pasta, bring a large saucepan of salted water with the vegetable oil to the boil. Place a large bowl of cold water near the cooker and lay some clean dry kitchen cloths nearby. When the water boils, drop in 5 or 6 rectangles of pasta and stir with a wooden spoon. Cook for 20 seconds after the water has come back to the boil and then lift each sheet of pasta out with a fish slice and plunge it into the bowl of cold water. Lift it out and lay it on the cloths. Repeat this operation until all the pasta is cooked. Pat the top of the lasagne dry.

If you are using bought lasagne, cook according to the directions on the packet.

Butter a large shallow ovenproof dish or a roasting tin in which the cannelloni will fit in a single layer.

Spread 30 ml/2 tablespoons of the meat mixture on each rectangle of pasta, leaving a 1 cm/½ inch border all around. Roll the rectangle up its narrow side. Lay the rolls in the dish with the folded-over edge facing downwards. The cannelloni can be packed quite tightly together.

Spread the béchamel sauce over the rolled-up cannelloni, sprinkle with the remaining Parmesan and dot with the remaining butter. Bake in the oven for 20 minutes until golden.

Allow to settle for 5 to 7 minutes before serving.

Tortelli di Ricotta e Spinaci   *Tortelli filled with ricotta and spinach*

EMILIA-ROMAGNA

If you can, buy Swiss chard instead of spinach, as it has a more delicate flavour.

Preparation time: 30 minutes (plus about
1–1½ hours for pasta making)
Cooking time: 10–15 minutes
Serves: 4 as a main course, 6 as a first
course

225 g/8 oz Swiss chard or spinach leaves,
or 150 g/5 oz frozen leaf spinach,
thawed
100 g/4 oz ricotta cheese
150 g/5 oz freshly grated Parmesan cheese
1 egg yolk
pinch of grated nutmeg
salt and freshly ground black pepper
pasta made with 3 eggs and 300 g/11 oz
flour (see page 139)
15 ml/1 tablespoon vegetable oil
100 g/4 oz butter

Cook the chard or spinach with a little salt over low heat, covered, for about 10 minutes if fresh or 5 minutes if frozen. Drain and when the spinach is cool squeeze out the moisture with your hands and chop finely. Put it in a bowl, add the ricotta, 50 g/2 oz of Parmesan, the egg yolk and grated nutmeg and mix well. Season to taste.

Make the pasta as directed on page 139. If you are making the pasta by hand, cut a strip 7·5 cm/3 inches wide, keeping the rest of the pasta folded into a loose roll and well covered with a cloth. If you are making the pasta by hand-cranked machine, roll out one strip at a time, keeping the rest wrapped in cling film.

Put heaped teaspoons of the filling down the centre of the strip, spacing them 2·5 cm/1 inch apart. Fold the strip over, pressing around each pocket of the filling with your fingers and cut between each pocket with a pastry wheel. Each *tortello* will have three cut edges. Repeat until all the ingredients have been used.

Put 4 litres/7 pints of water in a large saucepan, add 30 ml/2 tablespoons salt and the vegetable oil and bring to the boil. Drop in the tortelli, stir gently with a wooden spoon and cover until the water returns to the boil. Cook until *al dente*, firm to the bite.

When the tortelli are cooked, lift them out of the water with a large slotted spoon or a large strainer and put them into a heated dish. Put knobs of butter on top of each layer and sprinkle with the remaining Parmesan. Toss them very gently and serve at once.

Maccheroncini alla Sarda   *Macaroni with minted meat sauce*

SARDINIA

Mint is used sparingly in Italy, and only in two regions, Lazio and Sardinia, is it used much.

Preparation time: 15 minutes
Cooking time: 45 minutes
Serves: 4 as a main course

75 ml/5 tablespoons olive oil
1 garlic clove, crushed
225 g/8 oz chuck steak, cut into 2·5-cm/
1-inch pieces
30 ml/2 tablespoons red wine
500 g/1 lb tomatoes, skinned, or 396-g/
14-oz can plum tomatoes, with their juice
15 ml/1 level tablespoon tomato purée
salt and freshly ground black pepper
350 g/12 oz short tubular pasta, such as
ditali or small macaroni
25 g/1 oz butter
30 ml/2 tablespoons chopped fresh mint
40 g/1½ oz freshly grated Romano or
Parmesan cheese

Heat the oil in a large saucepan, add the garlic and sauté until pale golden. Add the meat and brown on all sides. Pour over the wine and boil rapidly for 3 minutes to reduce. Add the tomatoes, the tomato purée and the salt and pepper. Simmer, uncovered, for 45 minutes until the meat is tender.

Just before the sauce is ready, drop the pasta in rapidly boiling salted water and cook until *al dente*, firm to the bite. Drain and turn it into a warm bowl.

Add the butter and toss well. Cover with the sauce and sprinkle with the mint and half of the grated cheese. Mix thoroughly and serve at once, with the remaining cheese in a small bowl.

Ravioli alla Milanese *Ravioli Milanese style*

Ravioli originated from Liguria, but they are now made all over northern Italy, even if they may have different names from one region to another.

The stuffing used in this recipe is similar to the one my mother used to make in Milan for Sabato Grasso, just before Lent began. She would use a 225 g/8 oz piece of chuck steak, brown it quickly, then cover it with water and cook it very slowly for about 1½ hours, until the meat was tender. It would then be chopped finely and a little of the cooking juice would be added to the filling. For convenience, however, I have substituted mince in this recipe.

Preparation time: 20 minutes (plus 1–1½ hours for pasta making)
Cooking time: 10 minutes
Serves: 4 as a main course, 6 as a first course

75 g/3 oz butter
75 g/3 oz unsmoked bacon, very finely chopped
350 g/12 oz fresh best minced beef
150 ml/¼ pint meat stock (see page 138)
1 sprig of rosemary
salt and freshly ground black pepper
90 g/3½ oz freshly grated Parmesan cheese
1 egg
pinch of ground cinnamon
pasta made with 3 eggs and 300 g/11 oz flour (see page 139)
15 ml/1 tablespoon vegetable oil
5 fresh sage leaves, slightly crushed
1 garlic clove

To make the stuffing, heat 15 g/½ oz of the butter in a saucepan. Add the bacon and minced meat and fry for about 5 minutes until brown. Add the stock, rosemary, salt and pepper and simmer gently for 20 minutes, stirring frequently until tender. Discard the sprig of rosemary. Turn the meat into a bowl and leave to cool. Add 50 g/2 oz of the Parmesan, the egg and cinnamon. Mix well.

Make the pasta as directed on page 139. Working quickly, to prevent it from drying out, cut a straight line along the far side of the pasta with a fluted pastry wheel. In a straight line, 6·5 cm/2½ inches from the cut edge, put a teaspoon of filling at 4 cm/1½ inch intervals. While you do this cover the rest of the pasta with a cloth. Fold the far edge of the pasta towards you just far enough to enclose the lumps of filling. Using the pastry wheel, cut this ridge of stuffed pasta, away from the rest of the pasta, and then cut between each lump of filling to form small squares. Repeat until all the ingredients have been used. If the edges do not stick well, pinch them together lightly with moistened fingers. If you are making the pasta by hand-cranked machine, roll out, fill and cut one strip at a time, keeping the rest of the dough wrapped in cling film.

Drop the ravioli into a large saucepan of rapidly boiling salted water containing the vegetable oil. Cover the saucepan and quickly return the water to the boil. Uncover and cook for about 5 minutes, until they come to the surface. The timing differs according to the size and thickness of the ravioli, but 10 minutes should be the maximum.

While the pasta is cooking, melt the remaining butter in a small saucepan. Add the sage leaves, and the whole garlic clove. Stir for 1 minute, discard the garlic and pour the butter sauce into a warm serving bowl. Add the remaining Parmesan.

Drain the ravioli and turn them into the serving bowl. Toss them quickly in the butter sauce, and serve at once.

If you have any pasta left over cut it into small squares— it does not matter if they are of different sizes and use them in soups.

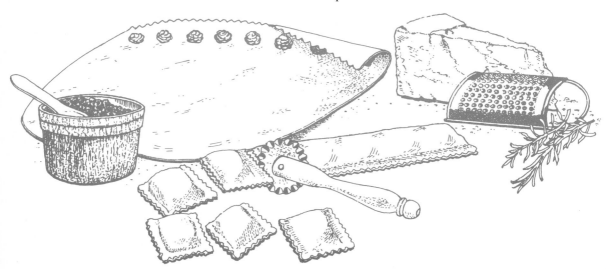

Pasticcio di Tagliatelle alla Boscaiola

Pasticcio of tagliatelle with mushrooms and eggs

VALLE D'AOSTA, PIEDMONT

Alla boscaiola means in the style of the woodman, and this dish is so-called because the species of mushrooms used— cèpes, russulas or chanterelles for example—are found in the mountain woods. Like most continental people I manage to find some wild species of edible funghi even in the outskirts of London and use these whenever possible. But I have also used cultivated mushrooms for this *pasticcio* and it still tastes excellent.

Preparation time: 15 minutes
Cooking time: 20 minutes
Oven temperature: 190°C, 375°F,
  Gas Mark 5
Serves: 4 as a main course

home-made tagliatelle made with
  400 g/14 oz plain flour, 2 eggs, about
  120 ml/8 tablespoons water and 5 ml/1
  level teaspoon salt (see page 139) or
  500 g/1 lb bought tagliatelle
2 slices of crustless white bread
45 ml/3 tablespoons milk
175 g/6 oz mushrooms, chopped
1 garlic clove
115 g/4½ oz butter
3 eggs, beaten
salt and freshly ground black pepper
50 g/2 oz Gruyère cheese, finely sliced
50 g/2 oz Bel Paese cheese, finely sliced
50 g/2 oz freshly grated Parmesan cheese
100 ml/4 fl oz double cream

If you are making your own pasta, follow the instructions on page 139, adding water to the eggs before mixing in the flour. Soak the bread in the milk for 10 minutes. Meanwhile sauté the mushrooms and the whole garlic clove in 90 g/3½ oz of the butter for 5 minutes and then discard the garlic.

Turn the mushrooms into a bowl and add the beaten eggs. Squeeze the milk out of the bread, mash it with a fork and add to the mushroom mixture. Season to taste and set aside.

Drop the pasta into rapidly boiling salted water and cook until *al dente*, firm to the bite. Drain, return it to the saucepan and toss with the remaining butter.

Pour half the tagliatelle into a large buttered ovenproof dish. Cover with the mushroom and egg mixture and with the sliced cheeses. Sprinkle with half the Parmesan and cover with the remaining tagliatelle. Pour over the cream, sprinkle with the remaining Parmesan.

Bake in the oven for about 15 minutes, until the top is golden brown. Allow to settle for 5 minutes before serving.

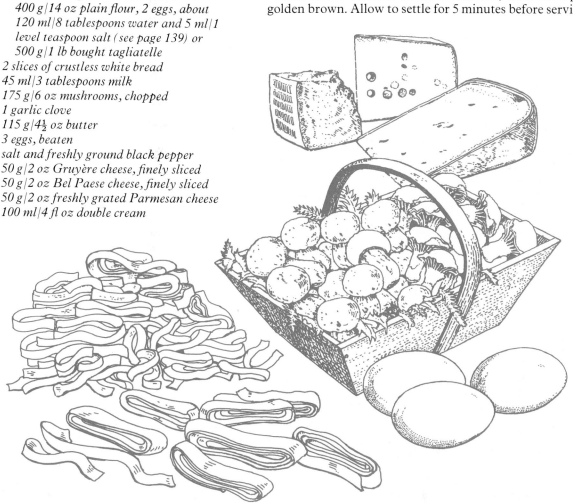

Pizza   *Pizza dough*

Pizza is not often cooked in Italian homes. It is eaten at a *pizzeria* after the cinema or as a snack before lunch with an aperitif. This is because domestic ovens are not as good for baking pizza as the old-fashioned brick varieties, and because there are so many excellent and quite cheap *pizzerias*!

A good pizza topped with fresh tomatoes and *mozzarella* and dressed with fruity olive oil is one of the greatest dishes of the Neapolitan cuisine. And even if it isn't quite as good as the one made in a baker's oven in Naples, you can certainly make a very tasty pizza at home.

Preparation time: 15 minutes (plus 2–3 hours rising)
Cooking time: 20–25 minutes
Oven temperature: 220°C, 425°F, Gas Mark 7
Serves: 2–3

Pizza dough:
15 g/½ oz fresh yeast or 7·5 ml/1½ level
    teaspoons dried yeast with 2·5 ml/½ level
    teaspoon sugar
200 g/7 oz plain flour
15 ml/1 tablespoon olive oil
5 ml/1 level teaspoon salt

Blend the fresh yeast in 100 ml/4 fl oz of warm water. If you are using dried yeast, dissolve the sugar in the water, sprinkle the yeast over and leave for about 15 minutes, until frothy.

Place the flour on a working surface, make a large well and pour in the dissolved yeast, the oil and the salt. Work in the flour with your hands to form a smooth ball and then knead until the dough is smooth and elastic, but not sticky.

Transfer the dough to a lightly floured bowl and cover with a damp cloth. Leave the bowl in a warm place for at least 2 hours, until the dough has doubled in size.

Pizza dough made in a food processor
Pour the flour and salt into the processor bowl. Start the processor and slowly pour the olive oil and the dissolved yeast into the bowl. Continue processing until the dough forms a thick mass. Remove the dough from the bowl and knead by hand for about 7 minutes, until smooth and elastic, and then leave to rise following the instructions above.

Pizza di Prosciutto Cotto e Funghi and Pizza Margherita

Pizza alla Marinara *Pizza with tomatoes and garlic*

pizza dough (see opposite page)
750 g/1½ lb tomatoes, chopped, or
   two 227-g/8-oz cans plum tomatoes,
   drained and coarsely chopped
5 ml/1 level teaspoon sugar
75 ml/5 tablespoons olive oil
3 garlic cloves, very finely sliced
10 ml/2 teaspoons oregano
salt and freshly ground black pepper

Make the dough according to the instructions opposite.

Put the tomatoes, the sugar and 45 ml/3 tablespoons of the oil in a saucepan and cook, stirring frequently, over a moderate heat for about 5 minutes, until soft. Place the sauce in a sieve, leave to drain for 5 minutes and then transfer the tomatoes to a food-mill and purée into a bowl.

Roll out the dough into a round about 25 cm/10 inches in diameter and, then with your fingers, make a slightly thicker outer edge. Transfer the dough to a lightly floured baking sheet.

Spread the tomato sauce evenly on the dough, sprinkle with the garlic, oregano, salt and pepper and pour over the remaining oil evenly.

Bake in the oven for about 20 minutes, until the edge of the pizza is crusty and golden brown.

Pizza Margherita *Pizza with tomatoes and mozarella cheese*

pizza dough (see opposite page)
1 mozzarella, weighing about 200 g/7 oz
75 ml/5 tablespoons olive oil
500 g/1 lb tomatoes, coarsely chopped or
   397-g/14-oz can plum tomatoes, drained
   and coarsely chopped
5 ml/1 level teaspoon sugar
5–6 basil leaves, coarsely chopped or
   5 ml/1 teaspoon oregano
15 ml/1 tablespoon freshly grated Parmesan
   cheese
salt and freshly ground black pepper

Make the dough according to the instructions opposite. Grate the mozzarella coarsely into a bowl and add 45 ml/3 tablespoons of olive oil. Leave to stand for at least 1 hour.

Put the tomatoes, the sugar and the rest of the olive oil in a saucepan and cook, stirring frequently, over a moderate heat for about 5 minutes, until soft. Place the sauce in a sieve, leave to drain for 5 minutes and then transfer the tomatoes to a food-mill and purée into a bowl.

Roll out the pizza dough into a round about 25 cm/10 inches in diameter and then, with your fingers, make a slightly thicker outer edge. Transfer the dough to a lightly floured baking sheet. Spread the mozzarella and the tomato sauce evenly over the dough and sprinkle with the basil or oregano, the Parmesan, salt and pepper.

Bake in the oven for about 20 minutes, until the edge of the pizza is crusty and golden brown.

Pizza di Prosciutto Cotto e Funghi *Pizza with ham and mushrooms*

pizza dough (see opposite page)
60 ml/4 tablespoons olive oil
1 garlic clove, lightly crushed
100 g/4 oz mushrooms, sliced
salt and freshly ground black pepper
100 g/4 oz ham, cut into matchsticks
30 ml/2 tablespoons freshly grated Parmesan
   cheese

Make the dough according to the instructions opposite.

Heat 15 ml/1 tablespoon of the oil with the garlic in a small frying pan. When the oil is hot, add the mushrooms, stir and, as soon as the oil has been absorbed, add the seasonings and lower the heat. Cook for about 5 minutes and then raise the heat and cook for a further 1 minute. Discard the garlic.

Roll out the pizza dough into a round about 25 cm/10 inches in diameter and then with your fingers make a slightly thicker outer edge. Transfer the dough to a lightly floured baking sheet. Spoon the mushrooms evenly over the dough, sprinkle with the ham and the Parmesan and pour over the remaining oil. Bake for about 20 minutes, until the edge is crusty and golden brown.

Pizzelle Fritte   *Fried small pizzas*

CAMPANIA

These little pizzas are made with the usual dough, but fried instead of baked. You can top them with any pizza topping, but I think this recipe is the best and the easiest to handle. The dough must be rolled out quite thin and then quickly fried in plenty of hot oil.

Preparation time: 30 minutes (plus 2–3 hours rising)
Cooking time: 10–15 minutes
Oven temperature: 200°C, 400°F, Gas Mark 6
Makes about 30

pizza dough (see page 50)
397-g/14-oz can plum tomatoes, drained and coarsely chopped
1 garlic clove, chopped
60 ml/4 tablespoons olive oil
salt and freshly ground black pepper
vegetable oil
60 ml/4 tablespoons freshly grated Parmesan cheese

Make the pizza dough following the instructions on page 50, adding 2·5 ml/½ level teaspoon extra salt.

Put the tomatoes, garlic, oil, salt and pepper into a saucepan and cook over a moderate heat for 10 minutes, stirring frequently. Pour the sauce into a sieve and leave to drain for about 5 minutes and then purée the tomato sauce remaining in the sieve into a bowl.

When the pizza dough has doubled in size, place it on the working surface and bang it to let the air out. Roll the dough out on a lightly floured working surface to a thickness of about 3 mm/⅛ inch. Using a 7 5-cm/3-inch round cutter, cut out as many circles as possible. Place the rounds on a clean tea towel while you cut out the rest. Knead the left-over dough, roll out and cut more circles.

Pour vegetable oil into a frying pan to a depth of 1 cm/½ inch. When the oil is hot, fry a few at a time for about 2 minutes on each side until golden. Drain the pizzelle on absorbent kitchen paper.

When all the pizzelle are fried, put them on a baking sheet, spoon a little of the sauce over each and sprinkle with a little Parmesan. Bake in the oven for 4 to 5 minutes until hot.

Serve immediately.

Calzoncelli   *Fried small folded-over pizzas*

CAMPANIA

These fritters are the miniature version of the baked folded-over pizza, the *calzone*. They are very attractive and, like *pizzelle*, make a delicious, original snack for a party. You can stuff them with any variety of stuffing. This is my favourite.

Preparation time: 30 minutes (plus 2–3 hours rising)
Cooking time: 15–20 minutes
Makes about 30

pizza dough (see page 50)
50 g/2 oz ham and 50 g/2 oz Italian salami, very finely chopped, or 100 g/4 oz mortadella, very finely chopped
50 g/2 oz mozzarella cheese, grated
30 ml/2 tablespoons chopped fresh parsley
15 ml/1 tablespoon freshly grated Parmesan cheese
1 egg
salt and freshly ground black pepper
vegetable oil

Make the pizza dough following the instructions on page 50, adding an extra 2·5 ml/½ level teaspoon salt.

In a bowl, mix together the ham and salami or the mortadella, the mozzarella, parsley, Parmesan, and egg. Mix thoroughly and add salt and pepper. Mix again.

When the dough has risen, place it on the working surface and bang it to let the air out. Roll the dough out on a lightly floured working surface to a thickness of 3 mm/⅛ inch. Using a 7·5-cm/3-inch round cutter, cut out as many circles as possible. Knead the left-over dough, roll out and cut more circles. Spread the ham mixture over one half of the circle, leaving a border at the edge. Wet your finger and moisten the edge and then fold the circles over and seal. Place them on a tea towel as soon as they are sealed while the rest are being prepared.

Pour vegetable oil into a frying pan to a depth of 1 cm/½ inch. When the oil is hot, fry a few at a time for about 2 minutes on each side, until golden. Drain on absorbent kitchen paper and, if you are serving the calzoncelli hot, keep them warm in the oven while you fry the rest.

Serve either hot or cold.

Calzone *Folded-over pizza*

CAMPANIA

When you hear people talking about *calzoni* in Italy, it is sometimes difficult to know whether they mean 'trousers', the literal translation of the word, or a type of pizza, folded over, which is very popular in southern Italy. *Calzone* fillings vary a lot, but unlike most pizzas, they never contain tomatoes. The dough can be made in a food processor (see page 50).

Preparation time: 30 minutes (plus 3 hours rising)
Cooking time: 12–15 minutes
Oven temperature: 230°C, 450°F, Gas Mark 8
Serves: 4

pizza dough (see page 50)
50 g/2 oz ricotta cheese
75 g/3 oz Italian salami, cut into 1-cm/½-inch cubes
100 g/4 oz mozzarella cheese, coarsely chopped
45 ml/3 tablespoons olive oil
salt and freshly ground black pepper

If you are using fresh yeast, dissolve it in 100 ml/4 fl oz of warm water. If you are using dried yeast dissolve the sugar in the same quantity of water and sprinkle in the dried yeast. Leave the yeast mixture in a warm place for 10 to 15 minutes until frothy.

Make the dough according to the instructions on page 50. Transfer it to a lightly floured bowl and cover with a damp cloth. Leave the bowl in a warm place for about 3 hours, until the dough has doubled in size.

When the dough is ready, break the ricotta into a bowl with a fork and add the salami, the mozzarella and 15 ml/1 tablespoon of olive oil. Season to taste.

Roll the dough out to make a 25·5-cm/10-inch circle and brush it with 15 ml/1 tablespoon of olive oil. Spoon the filling on to one half of the dough, leaving a 2·5 cm/1 inch border around the edge. Fold the dough over to form a half-circle and then push it into a crescent shape. With your fingers seal the edge and then make a pattern on it with a fork. Brush the remaining oil all over the top of the calzone.

Carefully place it on a baking sheet. Bake for 12 to 15 minutes until the calzone is golden. Serve it hot, with a bowl of Neapolitan tomato sauce (see page 132) if you wish.

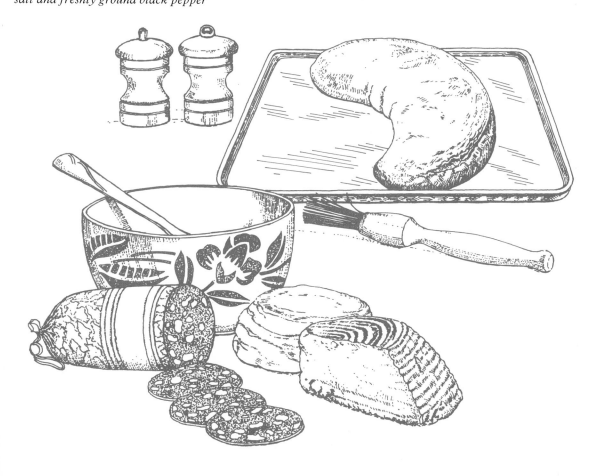

Pasta con le Sarde   *Baked pasta with sardines*

SICILY

This is one of the great dishes of Palermo, Sicily's capital, where it is made with fresh sardines and wild mountain fennel.

Preparation time: 20 minutes
Cooking time: 55 minutes
Oven temperature: 200°C, 400°F,
   Gas Mark 6
Serves: 4 as a main course

350 g/12 oz sardines with the heads and
   backbones removed
225 g/8 oz fennel bulbs, cleaned
100 ml/4 fl oz olive oil
1 onion, finely chopped
4 anchovy fillets, chopped
50 g/2 oz sultanas
25 g/1 oz pine nuts
a pinch of saffron, dissolved in 30 ml/2
   tablespoons warm water (optional)
salt and freshly ground black pepper
350 g/12 oz bucatini or spaghetti
30 ml/2 level tablespoons fresh dried
   breadcrumbs

Wash the fish and dry thoroughly with absorbent paper.

Drop the fennel bulbs into a large saucepan of salted boiling water and boil for 10 minutes. Drain, reserving the cooking water, and cut into thin short strips.

In a large frying pan, heat 90 ml/3½ fl oz of the oil with the onion and sauté for about 5 minutes, until soft and golden. Add the fennel strips, the fish and a few tablespoons of the fennel cooking liquid and cook for 10 minutes. Lift half of the fish out of the pan and set aside.

Meanwhile heat the remaining oil in a small frying pan, remove from the heat and add the anchovy fillets. Mash them up with a fork and keep warm.

Add to the frying pan containing the fennel and fish, the sultanas, pine nuts, saffron, the salt and pepper and cook for a further 5 minutes, stirring frequently. Add the anchovy mixture, remove from the heat and keep warm.

Meanwhile put the rest of the fennel liquid in a large saucepan, adding enough water to make up to 3·5 litres/6 pints of liquid. Bring to the boil and then add the pasta. Cook the pasta until *al dente*, firm to the bite. Drain and add it to the frying pan containing the fish and fennel sauce. Toss until well mixed.

Grease a deep ovenproof dish with a little oil. Pour half of the pasta into it, cover with the reserved whole fish and pour over the other half of the pasta. Sprinkle with the breadcrumbs. Bake in the oven for 15 minutes until the top has formed a golden crust.

Allow to settle for 5 minutes before serving.

Spaghettini con Salsa ai Filetti di Nasello
Spaghetti with fillets of whiting

PUGLIA

Preparation time: 15 minutes
Cooking time: 15 minutes
Serves: 4 as a main course

75 ml/3 fl oz olive oil
1 garlic clove, finely chopped
4 anchovy fillets
350 g/12 oz filleted whiting or hake,
   skinned and cut into small pieces
1–2 fresh chillies
350 g/12 oz tomatoes, skinned or 226-g/8-
   oz can plum tomatoes, with their juice
salt and freshly ground black pepper
15 ml/1 tablespoon chopped fresh parsley
350 g/12 oz thin spaghetti
25 g/1 oz butter

In a large frying pan, combine together the oil, garlic and anchovy fillets and reduce to a paste with a fork. Heat the mixture and then add the fish and the whole chillies. Sauté for 2 minutes, stirring frequently. Discard the chillies. Sieve the tomatoes, or purée in a liquidiser. Add to the fish and cook, uncovered, over a moderate heat for 10 minutes. Adjust the seasoning and stir in the parsley.

While the sauce is cooking, drop the pasta into rapidly boiling salted water and cook until *al dente*, firm to the bite, drain and turn into a heated dish. Toss with the butter and cover with the sauce. Serve at once.

Tortellini alla Panna *Tortellini filled with chicken and ham*

EMILIA-ROMAGNA

In Bologna these *tortellini* are usually eaten at Christmas and during Carnival week. They are cooked and served in a clear home-made stock.

This recipe is for *tortellini asciutti*, which means that they are cooked in water, drained and dressed either with butter and cheese, or with a tomato sauce, or with cream and cheese.

Preparation time: 1 hour (plus 1 hour for
pasta making)
Cooking time: 10 minutes
Serves: 4 as a main course, 6 as a first
course

50 g/2 oz butter
150 g/5 oz lean pork loin, sliced
150 g/5 oz chicken or turkey breast
50 g/2 oz mortadella, finely chopped
50 g/2 oz ham, finely chopped
2 eggs
pinch of grated nutmeg
150 g/5 oz freshly grated Parmesan cheese
salt and freshly ground black pepper
pasta made with 3 eggs and 300 g/11 oz
flour (see page 139)
15 ml/1 tablespoon vegetable oil
150 ml/¼ pint double cream

Melt 15 g/½ oz of the butter in a frying pan, add the pork and brown for 5 minutes. Add the chicken or turkey breast and cook for 3 minutes. Remove with a slotted spoon and leave to cool.

When the meat is cold, chop as finely as possible. Place in a bowl, with the mortadella, ham, eggs, nutmeg and 75 g/3 oz of Parmesan. Mix well and adjust the seasonings.

Prepare the pasta as directed on page 139. With a plain biscuit cutter, cut 24 rounds about 4 cm/1½ inches in diameter from the sheet of pasta dough. Cover the rest of the dough with a cloth. On each round put a small amount of the stuffing. Fold the round in half over the stuffing—the top edge should come just short of the bottom edge—and press down firmly to seal. Bring the two points of the semi-circle together, curling it round your index finger to form a ring and press the two points together to seal. As you make the tortellini lay them out on a dry, clean cloth. Repeat the same operation with another batch of 24 tortellini. Continue until all the pasta dough has been used. If you are making the pasta by hand-cranked machine, roll out, cut and fill one strip at a time, keeping the rest of the dough wrapped in cling film.

Put 4 litres/7 pints of water into a large saucepan or pre-serving pan, add 30 ml/2 tablespoons salt and the vegetable oil and bring to the boil. Drop in the tortellini, stir gently with a wooden spoon and cover until the water returns to the boil. Fresh tortellini cook very quickly. Taste 5 minutes after the water comes back to the boil: they should be cooked through but firm.

While the tortellini are cooking, put the remaining butter and half the cream into a small heavy saucepan and simmer for about 1 minute, until the butter and cream have thickened. Transfer to a heated serving bowl and place it in a very low oven to keep warm.

When the tortellini are cooked, lift them out of the water with a large slotted spoon or a large strainer and put them in the bowl with the cream and butter. Toss them and add the remaining cream and the Parmesan.

Serve at once. If you want, serve extra Parmesan separately in a bowl. If you want to serve the tortellini in home-made stock as a soup (see page 138), the above quantity is enough for 8 people.

If you have any pasta left over, cut into small squares—it does not matter if they are of different sizes, and use them in soups.

Frittata   *Italian flat omelette*

A *frittata* differs from a French omelette in being flat and round, not folded. It is also firm because the eggs are cooked over a low heat for at least 10 minutes.

The recipe below for *frittata* with cheese gives the basic cooking method, to which you can refer back when you make the other recipes.

Frittata al Formaggio   *Italian flat omelette with grated cheese*

EMILIA-ROMAGNA

Preparation time: 2 minutes
Cooking time: 15 minutes
Serves: 4

75 g/3 oz freshly grated Parmesan
salt and freshly ground black pepper
6 eggs, beaten
40 g/1½ oz butter

Add the grated cheese and the seasonings to the beaten eggs.

Melt the butter in a 25-cm/10-inch frying pan and, when the foam begins to subside, add the egg and cheese mixture. Turn down the heat and cook for 5 to 10 minutes until the mixture is firm and only the top is runny. Heat the grill and put the frying pan under the grill until the top is set, but not hard.

Loosen the frittata with a palette knife and transfer on to a round serving dish.

Frittata con le Cipolle   *Italian flat omelette with onions*

VENETO

Preparation time: 10 minutes
Cooking time: 25 minutes
Serves: 4

3 large onions, very finely sliced
30 ml/2 tablespoons vegetable oil
5 eggs, beaten
salt and freshly ground black pepper
40 g/1½ oz butter

In a large frying pan cook the onions in the oil over low heat until soft and golden. Lift the onion out of the pan and add to the beaten eggs. Season and mix thoroughly.

Cook the mixture in the butter as in the basic recipe.

Frittata con Mortadella e Mozzarella
Italian flat omelette with mortadella and mozzarella

CAMPANIA

Preparation time: 5 minutes
Cooking time: 20 minutes
Serves: 4

5 eggs, beaten
100 g/4 oz mortadella, cut into matchsticks
100 g/4 oz mozzarella, cut into matchsticks
15 ml/1 tablespoon chopped fresh parsley
15 ml/1 tablespoon freshly grated
   Parmesan cheese
salt and freshly ground black pepper
40 g/1½ oz butter

To the beaten eggs add all other ingredients except the butter.

Proceed to cook the mixture in the butter as in basic recipe, but for a little longer to allow the mozzarella to melt.

MEATS

Manzo con le Patate alle Acciughe

Beef and potatoes with anchovy fillets

LIGURIA

The meat is cooked very slowly, over a low heat. The taste of the anchovies impregnates the meat, giving it a slightly sharp touch. The potatoes, which finish cooking in the sauce, are quite delicious too. Do not worry if they break a little; it is not an elegant dish, but is so good that the looks do not matter too much.

Preparation time: 20 minutes
Cooking time: 2–2¼ hours
Serves: 6

30 ml/2 tablespoons olive oil
25 g/1 oz butter
3 slices unsmoked streaky bacon, finely
  chopped
1 kg/2 lb beef joint, topside or chuck steak
  in a piece, securely tied
pinch of grated nutmeg
salt and freshly ground black pepper
4 anchovy fillets, chopped
juice of ½ lemon
100 ml/4 fl oz meat stock (see page 138)
1 kg/2 lb potatoes, peeled and cut into 5-cm/
  2-inch pieces
15 ml/1 tablespoon chopped fresh parsley

Put the oil, butter, bacon and the meat into a flameproof casserole or large saucepan and cook over moderately high heat until the meat is well browned on all sides. Add the nutmeg, salt and pepper, anchovy fillets and the lemon juice and pour over the stock. Cover and cook on top of the stove over a very low heat for about 2 hours, until tender.

Meanwhile, after the meat has been cooking for 1½ hours, boil the potatoes until nearly done, but still firm. Drain them very well.

By the time the meat is tender the liquid left should come half-way up the joint. Remove the meat from the pan and keep warm. Skim the fat from the surface of the liquid. Reduce over high heat if the sauce is too thin. Adjust the seasonings and add the potatoes and the parsley. Mix well and cook until the potatoes are tender.

Cut the meat into 1-cm/⅓-inch slices and lay them on a dish, slightly overlapping. Pour over some of the sauce, serve the rest separately and arrange the potatoes around the sides of the dish.

Bistecchine alla Pizzaiola   *Thin beefsteaks in pizza sauce*

CAMPANIA

You can vary the *pizzaiola* sauce, some of which may be used to dress a first course of pasta, by adding anchovy fillets or capers instead of the olives.

Preparation time: 5 minutes
Cooking time: 20 minutes
Serves: 4

60 ml/4 tablespoons olive oil
2 garlic cloves, very finely sliced
550 g/1¼ lb rump or fillet steak, cut into
  four 1-cm/⅓-inch thick slices
salt and freshly ground black pepper
397-g/14-oz can plum tomatoes, with their
  juice
5 ml/1 level teaspoon sugar
100 g/4 oz large black olives, stoned and
  quartered
5 ml/1 teaspoon oregano

Heat the oil and garlic in a frying pan over a high heat and add the steak. Fry for 1 minute on each side, lift out and place on a heated dish. Season both sides with salt and pepper and keep warm.

Add the tomatoes and the sugar to the frying pan, mix well and cook, over medium heat, for 15 minutes. Add the olives and oregano, season with salt and pepper and cook for a further 5 minutes.

Return the steaks with their juices to the pan. Coat in the sauce and then serve at once.

Cotolette alla Milanese *Veal escalopes Milanese*

LOMBARDY

The general of the Austrian forces occupying northern Italy in the middle of the nineteenth century loved *Cotolette alla Milanese* and took the recipe back to Vienna, where it was named after its adoptive place of birth—*wiener schnitzel*—and became famous the world over.

Originally made with veal chops, I have substituted escalopes, which can be of Dutch veal, turkey or chicken, in this recipe.

Preparation time: 10 minutes
Cooking time: 10–15 minutes
Serves: 4–6

500 g/1 lb veal escalopes
salt and freshly ground black pepper
1 egg, size 2, beaten
150 g/5 oz fresh dried breadcrumbs
100 g/4 oz butter
15 ml/1 tablespoon vegetable oil
lemon wedges
chopped fresh parsley

If the escalopes are very large, cut them in half. Season the meat and coat with the beaten egg and then with the breadcrumbs. Press the crumbs firmly into the surface of the escalope with your hands and shake off any excess.

Heat the butter and oil in a large frying pan and when the butter foam begins to subside, place a single layer of escalopes in the pan. Fry on both sides until golden. The escalopes need only a few minutes cooking—a maximum of 3 minutes on each side. Place on a warm dish and keep warm while the rest are cooking.

Serve with lemon wedges and sprinkle with chopped parsley to garnish.

Cotolette alla Milanese

Brasato della Nonna Caterina   *My grandmother's braised beef*

PIEDMONT

This is one of my grandmother's dishes and it is delicious. You must cook the meat for a long time, so that it literally melts in your mouth. At home it was served with *polenta* or potato purée—either makes an excellent accompaniment.

Preparation time: 15 minutes
Cooking time: 2 hours 40 minutes to
   3 hours 10 minutes
Serves: 6

1·5 kg/3 lb chuck steak, or topside, in one
   piece
flour, seasoned
1 large onion
2 carrots
1 large celery stick
2 bay leaves
2 cloves
2·5 ml/½ level teaspoon ground cinnamon
75 g/3 oz butter
30 ml/2 tablespoons vegetable oil
150 ml/¼ pint dry sherry
100 ml/4 fl oz meat stock (see page 138)
salt and freshly ground black pepper

Lightly coat the piece of beef in seasoned flour.

Put the whole onion, carrots, celery, bay leaves, cloves, cinnamon, butter and oil into a heavy casserole and lay the meat on top. Brown the meat on all sides for 10 minutes. Add the sherry, raise the heat and boil briskly for 2 to 3 minutes. Add half the stock and salt and pepper to taste.

Cover with a tight lid or foil and simmer for 2½ to 3 hours, turning the meat over every half hour and adding the remaining stock if the sauce becomes too thick.

When the meat can be easily pierced with a fork, lift it out of the pan and keep warm. Skim the fat from the sauce (you can use it to fry potatoes) and discard the bay leaves. Purée the sauce, adjust the seasonings and keep hot.

Carve the meat into thick slices and arrange on a warm serving dish. Cover with some of the sauce and serve the remaining sauce in a sauceboat.

Manzo alla California   *Beef braised in milk and vinegar*

LOMBARDY

I used to find the name of this dish very puzzling. What could an American state have to do with this very traditional dish from Lombardy? Then one day, when driving north of Milan, I came across a small town called California and all was explained!

Preparation time: 5 minutes
Cooking time: 3 hours minimum
Serves: 6–8

150 g/5 oz butter
4 shallots or 2 onions, very finely chopped
30 ml/2 level tablespoons flour, seasoned
1·5 kg/3 lb beef, top rump or chuck steak
   in one piece
1 celery stick, chopped
3 medium carrots, chopped
75 ml/3 fl oz wine vinegar
450 ml/¾ pint milk
30 ml/2 tablespoons double cream
salt and freshly ground black pepper

Heat the butter in a heavy flameproof casserole and sauté the onion for 2 to 3 minutes until soft.

Meanwhile, spread the flour on a board and lightly coat the piece of beef with it.

Add the meat to the casserole and brown on all sides. Then add the celery and carrots and fry gently for 5 minutes, stirring frequently. Pour over the vinegar and boil rapidly to reduce slightly. Add the milk, bring to the boil, cover the pan with a piece of foil and then with the lid to seal it well, and simmer for about 3 hours, until the meat is very tender when pricked with a fork. Turn the meat two or three times during the cooking and add a few tablespoons of water if the sauce becomes too dry.

Remove the meat to a plate. Skim off excess fat from the sauce and purée in a liquidiser, food processor or through a sieve with the back of a wooden spoon. Return the sauce to the casserole and boil rapidly for 3 to 4 minutes to reduce. Add the cream, taste and adjust the seasonings.

Slice the meat into 1-cm/½-inch thick slices and lay them, slightly overlapping, on a heated dish. Cover with half the sauce and serve with mashed potatoes and the remaining sauce in a sauceboat.

Stracotto alla Napoletana *Neapolitan braised beef*

CAMPANIA

Traditionally, in Naples, the meat from this stew is served as a second course, preceded by a mountain of pasta dressed with some of the sauce.

Preparation time: 30 minutes (plus 3 hours marinating)
Cooking time: 3 hours
Serves: 6

1 garlic clove, crushed
2·5-cm/1-inch piece of fresh chilli, seeded and finely chopped
5 ml/1 teaspoon oregano
salt and freshly ground black pepper
75 g/3 oz pancetta or unsmoked streaky bacon, cut into thin strips
1 kg/2 lb topside or chuck steak in one piece, tied into a roll
30 ml/2 tablespoons vegetable oil
75 g/3 oz lard
30 ml/2 tablespoons tomato purée, diluted in 225 ml/8 fl oz warm water
397-g/14-oz can plum tomatoes, with their juice
25 g/1 oz flour
25 g/1 oz butter

For the marinade:
225 ml/8 fl oz red wine
1 medium carrot, sliced
1 celery stick, sliced
1 small onion, sliced
2 garlic cloves, crushed
1 bay leaf
sprig of parsley
1 clove
1·25 ml/¼ level teaspoon grated nutmeg
1·25 ml/¼ level teaspoon ground cinnamon
salt and freshly ground black pepper

Mix together the garlic, chilli, oregano, salt and pepper and coat the pancetta or bacon with this mixture. Thread the strips through the meat in several places, across the grain, with a larding needle, or with a knife and a blunt instrument, such as a chopstick. Put the meat in a bowl and cover with all the marinade ingredients. Leave for about 3 hours.

Lift the meat out and dry it well with absorbent kitchen paper. Reserve the marinade.

In a large frying pan, brown the meat on all sides in 15 ml/1 tablespoon of the oil over high heat.

Heat the lard and the remaining oil in a heavy flame-proof casserole, in which the meat will fit tightly. Add the meat and the marinade, raise the heat and boil rapidly until the liquid is reduced by half.

In the pan in which the meat was browned, stir the diluted tomato purée into the meat sediment at the bottom of the pan. Add to the meat together with the tomatoes and their juice. Bring to the boil, cover with foil and then with the lid, and simmer very gently for about 2½ to 3 hours until the meat is very tender when pierced with a fork. Check the meat once or twice during the cooking time and add a little water if necessary.

Place the meat on a carving dish or board and leave to cool for a few minutes.

Meanwhile purée the sauce in an electric blender or food processor, or rub through a sieve with the back of a wooden spoon and pour it into a saucepan. Mix the flour and the butter with a fork. Heat the sauce to simmering point and add the flour and butter mixture a little at a time, stirring continually. Boil for 2 minutes.

Remove the string from the meat and cut it into 1-cm/⅓-inch slices. Lay the slices, slightly overlapping, on a warm oval dish and spread a few tablespoons of the sauce over them. Serve the remaining sauce in a separate sauceboat.

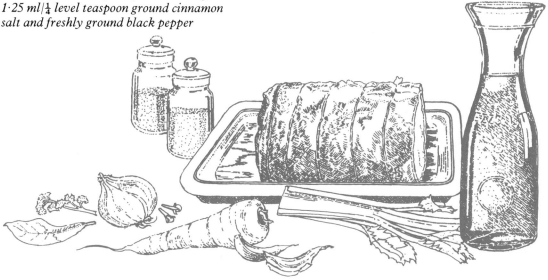

Osso buco   *Osso buco Milanese*

LOMBARDY

When you eat *Osso Buco* in Italian restaurants in Britain, you are usually served shin of veal swimming in tomato sauce. In fact the authentic recipe for this dish is without tomatoes. Ask your butcher for the hind shin, which is meatier and tastier than the front one. *Osso Buco* is usually served with *Risotto alla Milanese* (see page 111) and followed with a green salad.

Preparation time: 20 minutes
Cooking time: 2¼ hours
Serves: 4

1 onion, very finely chopped
65 g/2½ oz butter
15 ml/1 tablespoon vegetable oil
8 osso buco (veal shins), weighing about
  1·75 kg/3½ lb, securely tied around
  with string
45 ml/3 level tablespoons flour
salt and freshly ground black pepper
150 ml/¼ pint dry white wine
300 ml/½ pint meat stock (see page 138)
5 ml/1 level teaspoon grated lemon rind
½ garlic clove, very finely chopped
15 ml/1 tablespoon chopped fresh parsley

In a heavy frying pan, large enough to contain all the meat in a single layer and with a tightly fitting lid, gently fry the onion in the butter and oil for about 5 minutes, until soft.

Meanwhile coat the pieces of veal with the flour, shaking off any excess. Add the meat to the onion in the pan and brown well on both sides. Season with salt and pepper. Pour over the wine and boil rapidly for 5 minutes, turning the veal over several times. Add the stock, cover the saucepan and cook over very low heat for about 2 hours. Carefully turn and baste the osso buco every 15 minutes. If necessary add more stock during the cooking. If, by the time the meat is cooked, the sauce is too thin, remove the veal from the pan and reduce the liquid by boiling rapidly.

Mix together the lemon rind, garlic and parsley, to make the gremolada.

Remove the string from around the osso buco and serve piping hot with the sauce poured over the meat and the gremolada sprinkled on top.

Involtini alla Modenese   *Veal rolls stuffed with sausage and ham*

EMILIA-ROMAGNA

This recipe, from Modena, a town in Emilia-Romagna which rivals Bologna for the excellence of its food, requires *scaloppine*, very thin slices of Dutch veal cut from the scallop or the fillet of the veal. Ask your butcher to cut the *scaloppine* against the grain, so that they do not shrink and become tough during the cooking.

Preparation time: 20 minutes
Cooking time: 30 minutes
Serves: 4

500 g/1 lb veal escalopes, very finely sliced
100 g/4 oz luganega or other coarse-grained
  mild Continental sausage, cut into
  3·5-cm/1½-inch pieces
75 g/3 oz prosciutto
fresh sage leaves or dried sage
salt and freshly ground black pepper
50 g/2 oz butter
3 juniper berries, very slightly crushed
100 ml/4 fl oz dry white wine
30 ml/2 tablespoons veal or chicken stock

Beat the escalopes between two sheets of greaseproof paper, using a meat mallet or rolling pin, until they are very thin. Cut the veal into scaloppine, rectangles approximately 7·5 × 5 cm (3 × 2 inches). This quantity of meat should produce about 12 scaloppine. Cut the prosciutto into pieces 0·5 cm/¼ inch smaller than the veal slices.

Lay a piece of prosciutto, a piece of sausage and either a fresh sage leaf or a small pinch of dried sage on each scaloppine. Season with salt and pepper, roll up the scaloppine and secure each one with a cocktail stick.

In a large frying pan, melt the butter and place the veal rolls in one layer, add the juniper berries and fry briskly until brown, about 5 minutes. Add the wine and allow it to evaporate a little. Reduce the heat and add the stock, scraping the pan with a spoon to incorporate all the meat juices. Cover the pan and cook over gentle heat until the scaloppine are tender, about 10 to 15 minutes. Serve the meat and sauce together immediately.

Osso Buco and Risotto alla Milanese

Polpettone Casalingo *Meat roll*

VENETO

This recipe was given to me by a Venetian friend who is one of the best cooks I know. The meals she serves epitomise all that is good about Italian home cooking: excellent ingredients, prepared with the greatest care, and beautifully dressed.

Preparation time: 15 minutes
(plus 30 minutes chilling)
Cooking time: 1¼ hours
Oven temperature: 170°C, 325°F,
Gas Mark 3
Serves: 6–8

225 g/8 oz minced pork
225 g/8 oz minced chicken
300 g/12 oz minced beef
4 eggs
100 g/4 oz freshly grated Parmesan cheese
115 g/4½ oz fresh dried breadcrumbs
30 ml/2 tablespoons chopped fresh parsley
salt and freshly ground black pepper
90 ml/6 tablespoons vegetable oil
1 rosemary sprig
150 ml/¼ pint meat stock (see page 138)
45 ml/3 tablespoons dry white wine
15 g/½ oz butter
15 g/½ oz flour

Put the minced meats into a bowl with 3 whole eggs, the yolk of the fourth, the Parmesan, 75 ml/5 tablespoons of the breadcrumbs, the parsley and seasonings. Mix very thoroughly with your hands.

Shape the meat into a firmly packed ball, pat it to let any air out, and place it on a wooden board. Roll it out into a roll, about 8 cm/3 inches in diameter. Brush the surface of the meat loaf with the remaining egg white and coat evenly with breadcrumbs. Refrigerate for 30 minutes.

Heat the oil in a large flameproof oval casserole, add the rosemary sprig and the meat loaf and brown it on all sides, until a rich dark crust is formed.

Pour over the stock, cover and cook, over very low heat, for about 1 hour. Turn it over very carefully every 15 minutes and baste it often.

When cooked, remove the meat from the pan and place it on a wooden carving board. Let it cool a little before carving, then cut the meat into 1-cm/½-inch thick slices and place them, slightly overlapping, on a warm ovenproof dish. Pour 30 ml/2 tablespoons of the stock on to the meat, cover the dish with foil and put it in the oven for 10 to 15 minutes while you make the sauce.

Strain the stock into a saucepan and bring it to the boil, then add the wine and boil for 1 minute. Combine the butter and flour with a fork, and add this mixture to the sauce gradually, stirring all the time. Boil for 1 to 2 minutes. Serve the meat and sauce separately. The polpettone is also good served cold.

Rognoncini Trifolati all' Acciuga e Limone
Calf's kidneys in a sharp sauce

EMILIA-ROMAGNA

The verb *trifolare* describes the method of cooking meat or vegetables in olive oil, garlic and parsley. The word is derived from *trifola*, which in northern Italy means truffle.

Preparation time: 15–20 minutes
Cooking time: 10 minutes
Serves: 4

500 g/1 lb calf's kidneys, or pig's kidneys
and 30 ml/2 tablespoons wine vinegar
40 g/1½ oz butter, softened at room
temperature
15 ml/1 level tablespoon flour
4 anchovy fillets, finely chopped
45 ml/3 tablespoons olive oil
1 garlic clove, finely chopped
salt and freshly ground black pepper
15 ml/1 tablespoon chopped fresh parsley
10 ml/2 teaspoons lemon juice

If you use pig's kidneys, cover them with cold water and add 30 ml/2 tablespoons wine vinegar. Leave to soak for 30 minutes.

Split the kidneys in half, wash them under cold water and dry them with absorbent kitchen paper. Try to remove all the fat and as many white tubes as you can from the kidneys, then cut them into thin slices.

With a wooden spoon, blend together the butter, flour and the anchovy fillets and set aside.

Heat the oil with the garlic in a frying pan, add the kidneys and sauté until they begin to change colour, which will take only a few minutes. (It is very important not to overcook kidneys or they will become tough.) Lower the heat, and add the anchovy mixture very gradually, stirring constantly. Adjust the seasonings. Cook for 1 minute.

Turn off the heat, add the parsley and lemon juice and serve at once with *Patate Mascé* (see page 96) or with plain boiled rice tossed with a little butter.

Fegato alla Veneziana *Calf's liver with onions*

VENETO

A classic recipe from Venice, now well-known all over Italy and featured on the menu of many restaurants in Britain. It should be made with calf's liver, which is perfect in conjunction with the sweetness of the onion, but, if you cannot get it, use lamb's liver. Serve with fried *Polenta* (see page 110) or with mashed potatoes.

Preparation time: 10 minutes
Cooking time: 35 minutes
Serves: 4

50 g/2 oz butter
60 ml/4 tablespoons vegetable oil
500 g/1 lb onions, very finely sliced
500 g/1 lb calf's liver, very finely sliced
salt and freshly ground black pepper
15 ml/1 tablespoon chopped fresh parsley

Heat the butter and oil in a frying pan. Add the onions, mix well, and cook, very gently, for 30 minutes. The onion should be very soft and just coloured. Stir occasionally during the cooking, pressing the onions against the sides of the pan to release the juices.

When the onions are cooked, raise the heat and add the liver. Fry for 2 minutes on each side. Do not overcook; the liver should be pink inside. Season with salt and pepper and sprinkle with the parsley. Serve at once.

Braciole di Maiale Ripiene *Stuffed slices of loin of pork*

UMBRIA

This recipe from central Italy uses *fontina*, which is in fact not a local cheese, since it comes from Piedmont. If you can't find the Italian-made cheese, rather than use Danish *fontina*, which becomes tough when cooked, buy Gouda, which is slightly saltier, but a good substitute.

Preparation time: 20 minutes
Cooking time: 55 minutes
Serves: 4

750 g/1½ lb loin of pork, cut into 4 thin
  slices
50 g/2 oz minced veal
1 egg
30 ml/2 tablespoons freshly grated Par-
  mesan cheese
2 fresh sage leaves, chopped, or 2·5 ml/½
  teaspoon dried sage
pinch of grated nutmeg
salt and freshly ground black pepper
4 thin slices of mortadella
100 g/4 oz fontina or Gouda cheese, cut
  into thin slices
25 g/1 oz butter
30 ml/2 tablespoons vegetable oil
100 ml/4 fl oz dry white wine

Pound the pork slices until very thin and lay them flat on a wooden board. In a bowl, mix the minced veal, egg, Parmesan, sage and nutmeg well together.

Season the pork slices with salt and pepper and on each one place a slice of mortadella, a quarter of the veal mixture and a quarter of the fontina cheese. Fold the pork over and secure with a cocktail stick.

Heat the butter and oil in a frying pan, large enough to accommodate the stuffed pork without overlapping, and slide in the meat. Brown for about 5 minutes on each side, turning over carefully. Season with a little salt and pepper and pour over the wine. Cook, covered, over a gentle heat, for about 45 minutes, adding a little stock if the meat becomes too dry.

Serve piping hot.

Scaloppine di Maiale al Marsala   *Pork scaloppine with Marsala*

SICILY

Ask the butcher to cut very thin slices from a loin of pork. The dish can also be prepared with *scaloppine* of veal.

If you have no Marsala in the house, add 45 ml/3 tablespoons of lemon juice instead and sprinkle the *scaloppine* with 30 ml/2 tablespoons of chopped parsley just before serving. These are called *Scaloppine al Limone*.

Preparation time: 5 minutes
Cooking time: 5 minutes
Serves: 4

500 g/1 lb pork scaloppine
45 ml/3 tablespoons vegetable oil
1 garlic clove
salt and freshly ground black pepper
25 g/1 oz butter
15 g/½ oz flour
100 ml/4 fl oz Marsala

Pound the pork slices to a thickness of about 0·5 cm/¼ inch. Then cut each slice into small pieces no more than 8 cm/ 3 inch square.

In a frying pan, heat the oil with the garlic over moderate heat. When the oil is hot add the scaloppine and brown quickly on each side. Transfer them to a heated dish and season with salt and pepper. Keep warm.

Mix together the butter and the flour.

Remove the garlic from the frying pan and discard. Add the Marsala and boil rapidly for 5 seconds, stirring well to incorporate any sediment on the bottom of the pan. Add the flour and butter mixture, mix well and boil for 1 to 2 minutes.

Pour the sauce over the scaloppine and serve immediately.

Tagliatelle con Gulasch alla Triestina
Tagliatelle with goulash Triestine style

VENETIA-GIULIA, VENETO

As appetising as its Hungarian cousin, this goulash is ideal for dinner parties as it is actually improved by being made in advance.
Preparation time: 20 minutes (plus 1 hour
    for pasta making)
Cooking time: 1¼ hours
Serves: 4

50 g/2 oz lard or pork fat
50 g/2 oz butter
2 large onions, finely sliced
750 g/1½ lb pork fillet, cut into thick slices
30 ml/2 level tablespoons paprika,
    or more according to taste
15 ml/1 level tablespoon flour
15 ml/1 level tablespoon tomato purée
5 ml/1 level teaspoon grated lemon rind
salt and freshly ground black pepper
100 ml/4 fl oz red wine
2 large yellow or red peppers, seeded and cut
    into thin strips
2 large tomatoes, skinned and roughly
    chopped
225 ml/8 fl oz home-made meat stock (see
    page 138)
tagliatelle made with 300 g/11 oz flour,
    3 eggs (see page 139) or 400 g/14 oz
    bought tagliatelle

Heat the lard and half the butter in a saucepan, add the onions and sauté until soft, but not brown. Add the meat and brown well on all sides. Mix in the paprika, flour and tomato purée and cook for 1 to 2 minutes, stirring constantly. Add the lemon rind, salt and pepper.

Pour the wine over the meat and reduce by boiling rapidly for 2 minutes. Add the peppers and the tomatoes and mix well. Cover with the stock and simmer, tightly covered, for about 1 hour.

If you intend to eat the goulash the next day, leave it to cool and then place in the refrigerator.

Just before serving, uncover the goulash and reduce over high heat. The sauce should thicken and become velvety.

Meanwhile cook the tagliatelle until it is *al dente*, firm to the bite. Drain it, turn into a warm serving dish and toss with the remaining butter. Spoon over some of the sauce and serve at once, surrounded by the goulash.

Cima Ripiena *Stuffed breast of veal*

LIGURIA

Ligurian food, like this veal dish, is often elaborate and time-consuming to make. But the result—a plate of thin slices of tender meat with a very delicate stuffing—is well worth the trouble. The veal should be served without a sauce, accompanied only by a salad of French beans and tomatoes or of boiled courgettes sprinkled with parsley and dressed with olive oil; or simply a green salad.

*Preparation time: 1¼ hours (plus about
    2 hours cooling time)*
Cooking time: 2 hours
Serves: 8

100 g/4 oz calf's sweetbread
50 g/2 oz white bread, crustless
100 ml/4 fl oz milk
juice of ½ lemon
salt and freshly ground black pepper
1 small onion, finely chopped
25 g/1 oz butter
*100 g/4 oz pie veal, fat and skin removed
    and cut into very small pieces*
*25 g/1 oz pistachio nuts, blanched and
    skinned (optional)*
5 ml/1 teaspoon dried marjoram
1 egg
*75 g/3 oz peas, cooked, or frozen petits pois,
    thawed*
*45 ml/3 tablespoons freshly grated
    Parmesan cheese*
1 kg/2 lb boned breast of veal, trimmed
1 onion
1 celery stick
1 carrot
1 bay leaf
5 peppercorns
*2 litres/3½ pints home-made meat stock (see
    page 138)*

First prepare the stuffing. Wash the sweetbread under cold water. Soak it for about 30 minutes. Meanwhile, soak the bread in the milk for 15 minutes. Place the soaked sweetbread in a saucepan of water with the lemon juice and a little salt, bring slowly to the boil and simmer for 15 minutes. Refresh the sweetbread under cold water and drain. Remove as much of the membranes and skin as you can and discard. Cut the sweetbread meat into small pieces.

Sauté the chopped onion in the butter for 3 to 4 minutes until golden. Add the pie veal pieces and cook for 5 minutes, stirring frequently. Add the sweetbread and cook for a further 5 minutes. Add a little seasoning and remove from the heat. When cool, lift the meat out of the pan with a slotted spoon and chop finely.

Scrape the onion and butter left in the pan into a bowl and mix together with the chopped meat, the pistachio nuts, the marjoram, egg, peas, the bread with the milk squeezed out and the Parmesan. Taste and adjust the seasonings.

To stuff the veal, make a horizontal cut into the breast of the meat along the longer side, leaving the other sides uncut like a pocket. Gently push the stuffing into this pocket, not too tightly because it will swell while cooking. Carefully sew up the opening and any holes you might have made while cutting the meat.

Meanwhile, put the whole onion, celery, carrot, bay leaf and peppercorns into a large flameproof casserole or saucepan, cover with the stock and bring to the boil.

When the stock is boiling, gently lower the stuffed meat into the casserole. Lower the heat and simmer for 2 hours.

Lift the meat out of the pan, put it between two plates and place a weight on top. Leave until cold before slicing thinly.

Cima Ripieni

Agnello al Capretto   *Leg of lamb marinated in wine and vinegar*

UMBRIA

The Italian name of this dish is literally 'lamb kid's style'. This is because the marinating of the lamb in wine, vinegar, herbs and spices gives the meat a slightly gamey and stronger taste. It is an excellent way to prepare New Zealand lamb, which I find lacking in taste.

Preparation time: 15 minutes plus 24 hours marinating
Cooking time: 1¼–1½ hours
Serves: 4

the butt end of a leg of lamb, weighing about
*   1·25 kg/2½ lb*
15 ml/1 tablespoon vegetable oil
salt

For the marinade:
1 onion, chopped
1 garlic clove, crushed
1 sprig of parsley
1 bay leaf
1 sprig of rosemary
1 sprig of sage
15 ml/1 tablespoon olive oil
2 cloves
10 juniper berries, slightly crushed
10 peppercorns
150 ml/¼ pint red wine
75 ml/3 fl oz wine vinegar

To make the marinade, put the onion, garlic, parsley, bay leaf, rosemary, sage and oil into a saucepan and fry gently for 5 minutes, covered. Add the cloves, juniper berries, peppercorns, wine and vinegar and boil for 10 minutes over a very gentle heat. Leave the marinade to cool a little and then pour it over the lamb. Marinate for at least 24 hours, turning the meat over and basting as often as you remember.

The next day, dry the meat and strain the marinade, discarding the herbs and spices.

Put the vegetable oil in a flameproof casserole into which the lamb will just fit. Heat the vegetable oil and then put in the meat and brown very well on all sides to seal in the juices. Remove the meat from the pan and set aside.

Wash the casserole thoroughly to remove the slightly burnt oil and residues. Return the lamb to the clean casserole and pour over the strained marinade. Bring slowly to the boil, add salt to taste and cook, covered, until the lamb is tender, basting often. If you like lamb just pink, 1¼ hours will be enough, otherwise cook for an extra 15 minutes. Transfer the meat to a heated dish. Skim off excess fat from the sauce.

Serve the meat whole and carve it at the table. Accompany with a separate bowl of sauce.

Spezzatino di Agnello alla Genovese   *Lamb and potato stew*

LIGURIA

A very succulent dish from Genoa and, incidentally, one of the very few simple dishes from this city. Try to buy firm potatoes, such as Desirée, rather than King Edwards, which break during the cooking.

Preparation time: 20 minutes
Cooking time: 1 hour
Serves: 4

60 ml/4 tablespoons olive oil
1 kg/2 lb shoulder of lamb, boned and cut
*   into 5-cm/2-inch cubes*
1·25 ml/¼ teaspoon mixed spices
1 small onion, finely chopped
15 ml/1 tablespoon tomato purée
300 ml/½ pint meat stock (see page 138)
4 medium potatoes, cut into small pieces
bay leaf
salt and freshly ground black pepper

In a flameproof casserole heat the oil and brown the meat well on all sides. Add the spices and onion and cook for 7 to 10 minutes until tender. Then add the tomato purée, stock, potatoes and bay leaf. Season to taste.

Cover and simmer very gently for about 1 hour. If necessary, add a few tablespoons of warm stock to the sauce during cooking.

Serve at once.

Agnello al Rafano *Lamb in horseradish sauce*

VENETIA-GIULIA, VENETO

I have never come across horseradish in Italian cooking, except in this very good recipe from Friuli, where there is a strong Yugoslav influence.

Preparation time: 20 minutes
Cooking time: 1½ hours
Serves: 4

75 g/3 oz butter
30 ml/2 tablespoons vegetable oil
1 onion, sliced
2·5 ml/½ teaspoon dried thyme
3 bay leaves
90 ml/6 tablespoons wine vinegar
175 ml/6 fl oz meat stock (see page 138)
salt and freshly ground black pepper
1·75 kg/3½ lb shoulder of lamb, boned
   and cut into 2·5-cm/1-inch cubes, with
   fat and gristle removed
45 ml/3 level tablespoons horseradish sauce
   (not creamed)
60 ml/4 tablespoons chopped fresh parsley

Put 25 g/1 oz of the butter, the oil, onion, thyme, bay leaves, vinegar, stock and salt and pepper into a flame-proof casserole and bring slowly to the boil. Add the meat and cook, covered, over a moderate heat for about 1½ hours, until meat is tender. If the meat becomes too dry, add a few tablespoons of warm water during the cooking. When the meat is ready, there should be hardly any liquid in the pan. If there is too much liquid, turn up the heat and reduce.

Melt the remaining butter in a small saucepan, then add the horseradish and the parsley and cook, stirring constantly, for 30 seconds. Pour the horseradish sauce over the lamb, amalgamate it with the cooking liquid and turn the meat over once or twice. Taste and adjust the seasonings.

Trippa alla Senese *Tripe with tomatoes and vegetables*

TUSCANY

Tripe, which is delicious when properly cooked, is a great favourite all over Italy. This particular recipe is from Siena.

Preparation time: 20 minutes
Cooking time: 2½ hours
Serves: 4

1·25 kg/2½ lb honeycomb tripe
75 ml/5 tablespoons vegetable oil
25 g/1 oz butter
1 large onion, chopped
45 ml/3 tablespoons chopped fresh parsley
2 garlic cloves, finely chopped
2 celery sticks, finely sliced
2 carrots, finely sliced
1 sprig of rosemary, chopped
1 cm/½ inch piece of fresh chilli, seeded
   and finely chopped
397-g/14-oz can plum tomatoes, coarsely
   chopped, with their juice
150 ml/¼ pint chicken stock or ½ stock cube
   dissolved in the same amount of water
1·25 ml/¼ teaspoon mixed spice
salt and freshly ground black pepper
30 ml/2 tablespoons olive oil
45 ml/3 tablespoons grated Parmesan
   cheese

Rinse the tripe thoroughly under cold water. Bring a large saucepan of salted water to the boil and add the tripe. Cook, covered, for 15 minutes. Drain and place the tripe in a bowl. Cover with cold water and leave until cold, then cut it into 1 × 8 cm/½ × 3 inch strips.

Heat the vegetable oil and butter in a saucepan and add the onion and parsley. Sauté for 3 to 4 minutes until the onion is soft and slightly coloured. Add the garlic, celery, carrots, rosemary and chilli and fry gently for a further 5 minutes, stirring frequently. Add the tripe, the tomatoes and their juice, the stock, the mixed spice and salt and pepper. Bring slowly to the boil, cover, and simmer very gently for 2 to 2½ hours until the tripe is very tender. Stir often during the cooking, and add a little warm water or stock if the tripe is getting too dry and sticking to the bottom of the pan. When ready, add the olive oil and the Parmesan and stir well.

Serve piping hot.

Spezzatino di Agnello e Peperoni *Stewed lamb with peppers*

ABRUZZI-MOLISE

In Abruzzi-Molise this stew is served with a home-made pasta called *Maccheroni alla Chitarra*. The *chitarra*, or 'guitar', consists of a wooden frame with metal strings tautly pegged to it. The pasta sheet is laid on the frame and pressed through the strings with a rolling pin, producing long angular spaghetti. The pasta is tossed in some of the sauce and the meat served afterwards as an entrée.

Preparation time: 15 minutes
Cooking time: 1¼ hours
Serves: 4

750 g/1½ lb lamb fillet with all the fat
  and skin removed, cut into 2·5-cm/1-inch
  cubes
75 ml/5 tablespoons olive oil
4 garlic cloves, finely chopped
2 bay leaves
2·5-cm/1-inch piece of fresh chilli, seeded
  and very finely chopped
100 ml/4 fl oz dry white wine
3 yellow or red peppers, cut into thin strips
226-g/8-oz can plum tomatoes, with their
  juice
salt and freshly ground pepper

Sauté the meat in 15 ml/1 tablespoon of the oil, together with the garlic, bay leaves and the chillies, until brown. Add the remaining oil, heat, and then pour over the wine and boil rapidly for 2 minutes, stirring constantly. Add the peppers and the tomatoes and bring to the boil. Taste and adjust seasonings. Cover the saucepan and cook, over very low heat, for 1 hour.

If the sauce is too thin when the meat is ready, uncover the pan and boil rapidly to reduce. Discard the bay leaves and serve piping hot.

Spezzatino di Agnello e Peperoni

Cotechino con le Lenticchie *Cotechino with stewed lentils*

EMILIA-ROMAGNA

Cotechino is a type of sausage made in Modena which was known in Roman times—the historian Pliny writes praising its flavour. It is a large pork salami, wrapped in sausage casing and then salted for a few days. It is easily available in Italian delicatessen shops and is usually sold already cooked.

Preparation time: 10 minutes
Cooking time: 1 hour
Serves: 4

350 g/12 oz brown lentils
15 ml/1 tablespoon vegetable oil
50 g/2 oz pancetta or unsmoked streaky
  bacon, finely chopped
1 small onion, very finely chopped
4–5 sage leaves or 1·25 ml/¼ teaspoon dried
  sage
salt and freshly ground black pepper
1 cotechino, weighing about 500 g/1 lb

Wash the lentils and pick out any pieces of grit.

Put the oil and the pancetta in a heavy saucepan and heat for 2 minutes. Add the onion and the sage and sauté for 5 minutes. Add the lentils and as soon as they are well coated with fat, pour over 900 ml/1½ pints of boiling water. Cover and simmer for about 1 hour or until the lentils are soft, but still whole and nearly all the liquid has been absorbed. Add salt and pepper to taste.

While the lentils are cooking, prepare the cotechino. Place in a saucepan of boiling water and simmer gently for 30 minutes. Allow to cool a little and then cut it into 1-cm/⅓-inch thick slices. Serve surrounded by the lentils.

Vitello Tonnato   *Veal in tuna fish sauce*

PIEDMONT/LOMBARDY

This traditional dish is justly famous throughout the world for its unusual and delicious taste.

Preparation time: 30 minutes (plus 6 hours cooling)
Cooking time: 1 hour
Serves: 4–6

1 kg/2 lb fillet of veal or boned leg, rolled and securely tied
75 ml/3 fl oz dry white wine
75 ml/3 fl oz wine vinegar
150 ml/¼ pint water
1 small carrot
½ celery stick
1 onion stuck with 1 clove
sprig of parsley
salt and freshly ground black pepper
several whole black peppercorns
mayonnaise made with 2 egg yolks, 250–300 ml/8–10 fl oz olive oil, 15 ml/3 teaspoons lemon juice, freshly ground black pepper, no salt (see page 130)
198-g/7-oz can tuna, drained
4 anchovy fillets
15 ml/1 level tablespoon capers
lemon slices
black olives

Put the veal, wine, vinegar, water, the whole vegetables, parsley, salt and a few peppercorns in a saucepan and bring to the boil. Simmer gently for about 1 hour, until the meat is tender. Lift the meat out of the pan and set aside to cool. Place the cooking liquid and vegetables in a blender or food processor and blend together to form a purée.

Make a mayonnaise following the instructions on page 130, but do not add any salt because the anchovies and the cooking liquid should flavour it enough. Pound the tuna and anchovies together with a fork, or blend in a liquidiser or food processor and mix into the mayonnaise. Add the capers and freshly ground pepper. Thin the mayonnaise sauce to the consistency of thick cream with the puréed cooking liquid. Stir well, taste and add salt if necessary.

When the meat is cold, cut into 1-cm/⅓-inch slices and lay them, slightly overlapping, on an oval serving dish. Cover with the tuna fish mayonnaise and garnish with lemon slices and black olives.

Vitello Tonnato

Cassoeula   *Stewed pork and cabbage*

LOMBARDY

Made with Savoy cabbage instead of beans, *Cassoeula* is the Milanese answer to the French *Cassoulet* and is traditionally served with *Polenta*. Boil the trotters and rind a day in advance, so that the fat may be easily removed.

Preparation time: 20 minutes plus chilling
Cooking time: 4½ hours
Serves: 6

2 pig's trotters, split into quarters
   lengthwise
250 g/9 oz pork rind
30 ml/2 tablespoons vegetable oil
25 g/1 oz butter
1 large onion, chopped
400 g/14 oz boneless pork, cut into
   5-cm/2-inch cubes
1 large carrot, chopped
1 celery stick, chopped
1 garlic clove, chopped
salt and freshly ground black pepper
1·5 kg/3 lb Savoy cabbage, shredded into
   2·5-cm/1-inch pieces
500 g/1 lb luganega or other coarse-grained
   mild Continental sausage, cut into 5-cm/
   2-inch pieces

Cover the trotters and the pork rind with 1 litre/1¾ pints of water, bring to the boil and cook for 45 minutes. Remove the trotters and the meat, cut off the excess fat and chop the rind into 5-cm/2-inch squares and set aside. Allow the stock to cool, refrigerate and, when the fat has solidified on the surface, remove it and discard.

Put the oil, butter and onion in a large 4-litre/7-pint heavy saucepan or preserving pan and fry for 5 to 10 minutes until the onion is soft, but not brown. Add the trotters and the rind and sauté for 30 seconds. Add the pork and cook for 4 to 5 minutes, stirring frequently. Add the carrot, celery and garlic and sauté for a further 2 minutes and then cover with the stock from the trotters. Taste and adjust the seasonings.

Cook, covered, over very low heat for 3 hours, stirring every now and then and adding some hot water if the stew gets too dry.

Blanch the cabbage for 2 minutes, and drain well. Add it and the luganega to the saucepan, mix well and cook for a further 30 minutes.

Serve piping hot.

Salsiccia e Cavolo Rosso alla Bolzanese
Sausage and red cabbage from Bolzano

VENETIA-TRIDENTINA, VENETO

Bolzano is a town in Trentino, a northern province which belonged to Austria until the Great War. The language spoken there is German and the food shows very strong Austrian influences.

Preparation time: 20 minutes
Cooking time: 2 hours
Serves: 4

50 g/2 oz dripping
30 ml/2 tablespoons vegetable oil
2 large onions, sliced
500 g/1 lb luganega or other coarse-grained
   mild Continental sausage
150 g/5 oz pork rind or unsmoked bacon
30 ml/2 tablespoons red wine vinegar
500 g/1 lb red cabbage, cut into 1-cm/½-inch
   strips
25 ml/1½ tablespoons tomato purée, diluted
   in 350 ml/12 fl oz warm water
salt and freshly ground black pepper

Heat the dripping and oil in a heavy saucepan. Add the onion and fry gently for about 10 minutes, until soft. Meanwhile, cut the sausage into 4-cm/1½-inch pieces, the pork rind or bacon into 2·5-cm/1-inch squares and add to the pan. Fry for 5 minutes until the sausage is darker in colour. Pour in the wine vinegar, raise the heat and boil briskly for 1 minute. Add the cabbage and fry for a further 1 minute, stirring all the time. Pour in the diluted tomato purée, mix well, taste and add seasoning.

Return to the boil, stirring all the time, then lower the heat, cover tightly and simmer gently for about 2 hours. If the dish gets too dry, add a few tablespoons of warm water. Taste and adjust the seasonings.

Serve piping hot with Polenta, (see page 110) as is the tradition in Trentino, or with mashed potatoes.

POULTRY

Petti di Pollo Gratinati

Chicken breasts baked in breadcrumbs

VALLE D'AOSTA, PIEDMONT

Preparation time: 35 minutes
Cooking time: 15 minutes
Oven temperature: 220°C, 425°F,
  Gas Mark 7
Serves: 6

6 fresh chicken breasts, boned
1 egg, size 2, beaten
100 g/4 oz fresh dried breadcrumbs
50 g/2 oz butter
90 ml/6 tablespoons vegetable oil
béchamel sauce made with 568 ml/1 pint
  milk, 50 g/2 oz butter and 40 g/1½ oz
  flour (see page 133)
100 g/4 oz Gruyère cheese, thinly sliced
salt and freshly ground black pepper

Dip each chicken breast in the egg, then
the breadcrumbs and shake off any excess.
Heat the butter and oil in a frying pan
and, when hot, cook the chicken breasts
in a single layer. Turn them over when
they are brown and fry the other side.
Drain on absorbent kitchen paper.

Make the béchamel sauce. Put the
chicken in a large buttered ovenproof
dish and cover with the sauce. Place the
sliced Gruyère on top. Bake in the oven
for 10 to 15 minutes until a golden crust
forms on the top.

Allow to settle for about 5 minutes
before serving, with courgettes, if liked.

Petti di Pollo Gratinati

Pollo all'Aretina   *Chicken with peppers*

TUSCANY

Tuscan chickens can be compared to the French *poulets de Bresse* for their delicious taste and for the firm texture of their meat. Alas, one cannot get them here, so use the next best thing—fresh chicken, not frozen. You will also need fat red and yellow peppers, which give the sauce a slightly sweet flavour.

Preparation time: 20 minutes (plus 1 hour marinating)
Cooking time: 45 minutes
Serves: 6

150 ml/¼ pint dry red wine
3 garlic cloves, crushed
500 g/1 lb tomatoes, skinned, or 397-g/
    14-oz can plum tomatoes, drained and
    sieved
6 fresh chicken joints, cut in half
½ lemon, cut into wedges
salt and freshly ground black pepper
100 ml/4 fl oz olive oil
1 small onion or 2 shallots, very finely
    chopped
15 ml/1 tablespoon chopped fresh basil or
    chopped fresh parsley
4 large red or yellow peppers, cut into thin
    strips

Pour the wine into a bowl, add the garlic and leave for at least 1 hour.

If using fresh tomatoes, quarter them and use a teaspoon to remove the seeds. Sieve the seeds, and reserve the juice. Roughly chop the flesh and set aside while you brown the chicken.

Rub the chicken joints with lemon and season with salt and pepper. Heat all but 15 ml/1 tablespoon of the oil in a large frying pan and, when hot, fry the chicken joints on both sides until golden and crisp. Transfer to a large shallow flameproof casserole and keep warm.

Turn the heat under the frying pan to high and evaporate nearly all the liquid released by the chicken joints. Then add the onion and sauté for 2 to 3 minutes until golden. Pour over three-quarters of the wine and garlic mixture, add the tomatoes with their juice and the basil or parsley. Cook over moderate heat for 10 minutes, stirring occasionally. Taste and adjust the seasonings.

Pour the sauce over the chicken in the casserole, and cook, covered, for about 30 minutes, until the chicken is just tender.

While the chicken is cooking, heat the remaining oil in a large frying pan and add the peppers. Mix well, add salt and pepper and cook gently for 20 minutes, stirring frequently to prevent from sticking.

When the chicken is just tender, add the remaining wine and garlic mixture and cook, uncovered, over moderate heat for 10 minutes. Then add the peppers, turning them in the sauce, and cook for a further 5 minutes. Serve piping hot.

Pollo alla Panna   *Chicken with cream*

LOMBARDY

This dish is not very well known outside Milan, but it deserves a wider reputation, since it is so delicious and yet so easy to prepare.

Preparation time: 10 minutes
Cooking time: 1 hour
Oven temperature: 200°C, 400°F,
    Gas Mark 6
Serves: 4

4 large fresh chicken joints, cut in half
25 g/1 oz butter
salt and freshly ground black pepper
150 ml/¼ pint double cream
30 ml/2 tablespoons chopped fresh parsley

Wash and dry the chicken pieces thoroughly. Heat the butter in a large flameproof casserole and, when the foam begins to subside, add the chicken pieces. Brown them quickly until they are a light golden colour on each side.

Season the chicken with salt and pepper and pour over the cream. Cover and bake in the oven for about 45 minutes–1 hour, until tender, turning the chicken pieces over twice during the cooking.

Serve sprinkled with the chopped parsley.

Pollo in Potacchio   *Chicken with tomato and rosemary sauce*

MARCHE

Potacchio is the name of a sauce added to chicken, rabbit or fish for a final cooking. The rosemary in this sauce will perfume your kitchen when the dish is cooking, as well as sharpen appetites!

Preparation time: 10 minutes
Cooking time: 40 minutes
Oven temperature: 200°C, 400°F,
*   Gas Mark 6*
Serves: 4

4 large fresh chicken joints, cut in half
½ lemon, cut into wedges
45 ml/3 tablespoons vegetable oil
50 g/2 oz butter
2 garlic cloves, finely chopped
1 onion, roughly chopped
salt and freshly ground black pepper
100 ml/4 fl oz dry white wine

For the potacchio:
2 shallots or 1 small onion, very finely
*   chopped*
3 sprigs of rosemary (12 cm/5 inches long),
*   very finely chopped*
45 ml/3 tablespoons olive oil
500 g/1 lb tomatoes, skinned, or a 397-g/
*   14-oz can plum tomatoes, drained*
½–1 dry chilli or 1-cm/½-inch piece of
*   fresh chilli, according to taste, seeded*
*   and very finely chopped*
salt

Wash and dry the chicken pieces thoroughly. Rub each piece with lemon.

Heat the oil and butter in a large flameproof casserole. Add the garlic, onion and chicken pieces and fry for about 5 minutes on each side until pale golden. Season with salt and pepper. Remove the chicken from the pan and keep warm.

Pour off most of the fat left in the casserole. Add the wine and boil rapidly for 1 minute. Add 30 ml/2 tablespoons of warm water and boil over high heat, scraping up the sediment left on the bottom of the casserole with a spoon. Taste and adjust the seasonings. Return the chicken pieces to the dish. Cover and cook in the oven for 20 minutes.

Meanwhile prepare the sauce. In a saucepan, fry the shallots and the rosemary gently in the olive oil for 5 minutes. Add the tomatoes, roughly chopped, and the chilli and salt to taste. Cook, uncovered, over low heat for 15 minutes. Adjust the seasonings.

By the time the sauce is ready, the chicken should have been removed from the oven. Pour the potacchio sauce over the chicken, amalgamate with the sediment in the casserole and return, covered, to the oven for a further 15 minutes until tender. Test by pricking a drumstick with the point of a sharp knife or a skewer. The juices should run clear. Serve piping hot with new or mashed potatoes.

Pollo alla Cacciatora *Chicken with rosemary and vinegar*

UMBRIA

This recipe is typical of the cooking of central Italy in that it is simple but all the different tastes are well defined. It is also cooked in a way that requires very little fat, which accentuates the particular freshness of the ingredients.

Preparation time: 15 minutes
Cooking time: 40 minutes
Serves: 4

30 ml/2 tablespoons wine vinegar
a sprig of rosemary (7·5 cm/3 inches long), chopped
salt and freshly ground black pepper
4 fresh chicken leg joints, cut in half
½ lemon, cut into wedges
30 ml/2 tablespoons olive oil

Put the vinegar into a glass, add 15 ml/1 tablespoon of water, the rosemary, and salt and pepper. Leave aside while cooking the chicken.

Wash and dry the chicken pieces, rub with the lemon, and season with salt and pepper. Heat the oil in a large frying pan and, when hot, add the chicken pieces. Cook, uncovered, over a moderate heat for about 35 minutes until the meat is tender, turning the chicken over frequently during the cooking. The skin of the chicken should be golden brown and crisp.

When the chicken is cooked, remove the pan from the heat. When the fat has stopped sizzling, pour over the vinegar infusion and return to the heat. Boil rapidly to reduce the liquid for about 5 minutes, then serve at once.

Pollo alla Cacciatora and Fagiolini alla Fiorentina (see page 95)

Pollo alla Marengo *Chicken cooked in brandy and tomatoes*

PIEDMONT

Marengo, in the south of Piedmont, is where Napoleon won one of his fiercest battles against the Austrians. While camping there, his chef created this recipe, out of the ingredients at hand.

Preparation time: 20 minutes
Cooking time: 1 hour
Serves: 4

4 fresh chicken joints
½ lemon, cut into wedges
50 g/2 oz flour
100 ml/4 fl oz vegetable oil
50 g/2 oz butter
30 ml/2 tablespoons brandy
salt and freshly ground black pepper
500 g/1 lb tomatoes, skinned, or 397-g/
*   14-oz can plum tomatoes, with their juice*
1 garlic clove, crushed
150 ml/¼ pint chicken stock
100 g/4 oz button mushrooms
4 slices of white bread, halved
30 ml/2 tablespoons chopped fresh parsley

Wash and dry the chicken joints, rub all over with the lemon and coat in the flour. Heat the oil in a large frying pan and brown the chicken joints on both sides, until golden brown, about 5 to 10 minutes. Remove from the frying pan and place, skin side up, in a large saucepan or flameproof casserole together with 25 g/1 oz of the butter. (Do not wash the frying pan or discard the remaining oil because it will be used later.) Sprinkle the chicken joints with the brandy and seasonings and turn the joints over. Roughly chop the tomatoes and add them and the garlic and stock to the chicken. Cover and simmer gently for about 1 hour, until the meat is tender.

Ten minutes before serving, melt the remaining butter in a pan and cook the mushrooms for about 5 minutes, until soft. Drain and add to the chicken.

Meanwhile reheat the oil remaining in the frying pan, add the slices of bread and fry on both sides until golden brown.

When the chicken is cooked (test by pricking a drumstick with a skewer—the juice which comes out should be clear), add the parsley and stir. Adjust the seasonings.

Remove the chicken joints to a heated serving dish. If the sauce is too thin boil briskly to reduce. Spoon the sauce over the chicken and serve garnished with the fried bread.

Fagiano alla Milanese *Pheasant in the fashion of Milan*

LOMBARDY

As I am from Milan, I naturally claim that the cooking of my native city is the best in Italy. Certainly it is one of the most sophisticated, and many of the dishes, such as *Fagiano alla Milanese*, reflect the strong influence of French cooking.

Preparation time: 20 minutes
Cooking time: 1¼ hours
Serves: 2–3

1 cock pheasant, plucked, trussed and well
*   hung, plus giblets*
salt and freshly ground black pepper
50 g/2 oz butter
25 g/1 oz pancetta or unsmoked streaky
*   bacon, cut into strips*
50 g/2 oz calf's liver, roughly chopped
100 g/4 oz lean pork, cut into small pieces
1 shallot or small onion, stuck with a clove
pinch of ground cinnamon
pinch of grated nutmeg
pinch of mixed spice
150 ml/¼ pint meat stock (see page 138)
150 ml/¼ pint dry white wine
30 ml/2 tablespoons single cream

Season the pheasant inside and out. Place in a flameproof casserole with the butter and the pancetta and fry for about 10 minutes, until brown on all sides. Add the calf's liver, pork, the pheasant giblets, cut into small pieces, the whole onion, the spices and salt and pepper. Pour over the stock and the wine.

Lower the heat, cover and simmer, for about 1 hour until the bird is tender. Remove the pheasant from the pan and keep warm.

Purée the sauce by rubbing it through a sieve with a wooden spoon or putting it through a food mill. Return it to a clean saucepan, bring to the boil and reduce rapidly for about 5 minutes. Remove from the heat. Add the cream, stir and keep warm over a very low heat. Do not allow to boil or the sauce will curdle.

Carve the pheasant and lay it on a warm dish. Spoon over a little of the sauce and serve the remaining sauce separately. Fried polenta is a perfect accompaniment (see page 110).

Tacchino Ripieno Arrosto *Stuffed turkey*

LOMBARDY

Turkey is the traditional Christmas fare in northern Italy, as in Britain. The Christmas dinner we used to have at home consisted of an antipasto of *bresaola* (fillet of beef specially cured then dressed with olive oil and lemon juice), *Risotto alla Milanese*, turkey stuffed with meat and fruit (as in this recipe), accompanied by roast potatoes and spinach cooked in the Roman fashion, followed by *soncino*—corn lettuce. There were lots of different desserts: *Panettone*, the traditional Milanese cake in the shape of a dome, *Torrone*, hard nougat from Cremona, éclairs and *Cannoli Ripieni* (cones of puff-pastry filled with egg custard or crème Chantilly). Then there were nuts and dates and dried figs, and big bowls of beautiful mandarines, Sicilian oranges, *zibibbo*—a grape originally brought to Sicily by the Arabs—apples and pears.

Preparation time: 1 hour
Cooking time: 3½ hours
Oven temperature: 180°C, 350°F,
  Gas Mark 4
Serves: 12

225 g/8 oz chestnuts
50 g/2 oz prunes, soaked
50 g/2 oz pancetta or unsmoked streaky
  bacon, cut into thin strips
175 g/6 oz butter
50 g/2 oz minced veal
50 g/2 oz luganega, or other coarse-grained
  mild continental sausage, skinned
1 turkey, weighing about 5–6 kg/11–12½ lb
  (undressed weight), with the liver
  reserved
1·25 ml/¼ teaspoon grated nutmeg
salt and freshly ground black pepper
1 dessert apple, peeled and chopped
1 pear, peeled and chopped
50 g/2 oz walnuts, finely chopped
15 ml/1 tablespoon brandy
1 onion, sliced
2 sprigs of rosemary
15 ml/1 level tablespoon flour
150 ml/¼ pint dry white wine

Make a horizontal cut all the way round the chestnuts, put them in a saucepan, cover with lots of cold water, bring to the boil and cook, covered, for 25 minutes. Peel the chestnuts and also remove the inner skin as soon as they are cool enough to handle, lifting them out of the water a few at a time. Finely chop the chestnuts and set aside.

Cook the prunes in boiling water for about 10 minutes, until they are soft enough for the stones to be removed. Chop the flesh finely and set aside.

Put the pancetta and 50 g/2 oz of butter in a frying pan and add the veal, the sausage and the chopped liver from the turkey. Sauté for 2 to 3 minutes, and then add the nutmeg and the seasonings. Mix well and turn into a bowl.

Add the apple, the pear, the prunes, walnuts, chestnuts and brandy to the meat mixture and mix well with your hands.

Stuff the neck end of the turkey with this mixture and sew up. If necessary tie the neck end with string or secure with skewers. Sprinkle the turkey generously with salt and pepper and rub 75 g/3 oz of the butter all over it. Put the sliced onion and the rosemary on a large piece of foil, place the turkey on top and fold it over to seal.

Lay the turkey on its side in a roasting tin and cook in the oven for about 2½ hours, turning the bird to the other side half way through the cooking. Remove the foil, lay the turkey on its back and cook for a further 30 minutes or until the meat is tender and the breast is crisp and brown.

Remove the bird from the tin and place it on a heated serving dish. Turn off the oven and put the dish in the oven, leaving the door ajar.

Work the flour into the remaining butter with a fork. Pour off most of the fat left in the baking tin and add the wine. Boil rapidly for 3 minutes. Remove from the heat and very gradually add the flour and butter mixture. Stir until smooth and then bring gently back to the boil. Taste and adjust the seasonings.

Slice the turkey and arrange on a serving dish. Serve the sauce separately.

FISH AND
SHELLFISH

Sfogi in Saor *Sole in sweet and sour sauce*

VENETO

The taste of this sauce in which the sole is marinated for two days, is strongly reminiscent of Middle Eastern cooking, like many other Venetian dishes. This is one of the dishes eaten in Venice during the Feast of the Redeemer.

Preparation time: 30 minutes (plus 2 days marinating)
Cooking time: 45 minutes
Serves: 4

500 g/1 lb sole fillets, cut in half lengthways
25 g/1 oz flour
salt and freshly ground black pepper
150 ml/¼ pint olive oil
1 carrot, very finely sliced
1 onion, very finely sliced
1 celery stick, thinly sliced
45 ml/3 tablespoons dry white wine
45 ml/3 tablespoons wine vinegar
50 g/2 oz sultanas
2·5 ml/½ level teaspoon ground cinnamon
2 cloves
2 bay leaves

Coat each fillet in the flour, seasoned with salt and pepper, and shake to remove excess. Heat 100 ml/4 fl oz of the oil in a frying pan. When hot, slide in the fillets a few at a time and fry gently for about 5 minutes on each side, until golden. Drain the fish on absorbent kitchen paper and then place in a shallow serving dish large enough to hold them all in a single layer.

Heat the remaining oil in a frying pan and sauté the vegetables for about 15 minutes, until soft and slightly coloured. Season with salt and pepper and add the wine and vinegar. Raise the heat and cook until the liquid is reduced by half. Pour over the fish and sprinkle with the sultanas, cinnamon, cloves and the bay leaves.

Cover the dish and refrigerate for 48 hours.

An hour before serving remove the dish from the refrigerator to return it to room temperature.

Sogliole Gratinate *Sole baked in breadcrumbs*

LIGURIA

This dish originates from the extreme western corner of Liguria near the border with France, and its flavour is evocative of Provençal cuisine.

Preparation time: 15 minutes
Cooking time: 35 minutes
Oven temperature: 190°C, 375°F,
  Gas Mark 5
Serves: 4

450 ml/¾ pint dry white wine
40 g/1½ oz butter
salt and freshly ground black pepper
30 ml/2 level tablespoons French mustard
15 ml/1 tablespoon wine vinegar
1 garlic clove, finely chopped
2 shallots or 1 small onion, finely chopped
1 tomato, skinned, seeded and chopped
4 lemon sole (each weighing about
  175 g/6 oz), cleaned, with heads still on
2 egg yolks
30 ml/2 tablespoons lemon juice
45 ml 3 level tablespoons fresh dried
  breadcrumbs
15 ml/1 tablespoon chopped fresh parsley

Boil the wine with 15 g/½ oz of the butter and salt and pepper for 5 minutes, then add the mustard, vinegar, garlic, shallots and tomato and cook for a further 10 minutes. Set aside.

Dry the sole and season inside and out.

Melt the remaining butter in the oven in an ovenproof dish large enough to hold the sole in a single layer. Place the sole in the dish and pour over the wine sauce. Bake in the oven for 15 minutes.

Remove from the oven, pour off the liquid and strain it through a sieve into a bowl. Stir in the egg yolks and lemon juice, mix well and spoon the sauce over the fish. Sprinkle with the breadcrumbs.

Turn the oven up to 230°C, 450°F, Gas Mark 8 and return the dish to the oven for a further 5 minutes to brown the top. Alternatively the fish can be browned under the grill.

Sprinkle with the parsley just before serving.

Pagello con i Funghi Trifolati   *Red bream with sautéed mushrooms*

ABRUZZI-MOLISE

Red bream is appreciated much more in Italy and France than it is here. It looks beautiful, with firm white flesh, and has a delicate taste, which in this recipe is enhanced by the mushroom sauce.

Preparation time: 10 minutes
Cooking time: 35 minutes
Serves: 4

225 g/8 oz mushrooms, sliced
2 large garlic cloves, finely chopped
75 ml/5 tablespoons olive oil
40 g/1½ oz butter
salt and freshly ground pepper
15 ml/1 tablespoon chopped fresh parsley
1 small onion, very finely chopped
5 ml/1 level teaspoon anchovy paste
1 bay leaf
75 ml/5 tablespoons white wine
1 red bream, weighing about 1kg/2 lb,
   gutted but with head and tail on
150 ml/¼ pint home-made meat stock (see
   page 138)

In a frying pan, sauté the mushrooms and half the garlic in 45 ml/3 tablespoons of the oil and 15 g/½ oz of the butter, over moderate heat. When the mushrooms have absorbed the oil, turn the heat to low and season with salt and pepper. Shake the pan and cook for 1 minute. Turn the heat up to high and cook for 5 minutes, stirring frequently. Add the parsley and adjust the seasoning. Set aside while you cook the fish.

In a flameproof dish, fry the onion gently in the remaining oil and butter for 2 to 3 minutes until soft. Stir in the anchovy paste, bay leaf and remaining garlic and cook for 1 minute, stirring. Add the wine and boil briskly until reduced by half, then add the fish, the stock and seasoning to taste. Cook, covered, for 10 minutes, then turn the fish over very carefully and cook for a further 15 minutes.

Mix the mushrooms into the liquid surrounding the fish and warm through for about 1 minute. Serve hot with new potatoes.

Nasello alla Siracusana   *Baked hake with anchovy sauce*

SICILY

The origins of Italian cooking are partly Greek and this influence is particularly strong in many of the recipes for cooking fish, like this one.

Preparation time: 10 minutes
Cooking time: 25–35 minutes
Oven temperature: 190°C, 375°F,
   Gas Mark 5
Serves: 4

1–1·5 kg/2–3¼ lb whole hake, cleaned and
   boned, with head and tail still on
60 ml/4 tablespoons olive oil
salt and freshly ground black pepper
2 sprigs of rosemary
½ lemon, cut into thin slices
5 salted anchovies, boned and rinsed,
   or 10 anchovy fillets
1 garlic clove, finely chopped

Wash the hake and dry well on absorbent kitchen paper. Brush a little oil inside the fish and season the fish cavity with salt and pepper. Put the rosemary and lemon slices inside and secure with a cocktail stick.

Heat the remaining oil in a small saucepan, add the salted anchovies or the anchovy fillets and the garlic and mash to a paste with a fork.

Lay the hake on a piece of foil which is large enough to wrap the fish in. Pour over the anchovy sauce, turning the fish over so that it is completely coated. Add a little salt and a generous amount of pepper. Fold over the foil, completely sealing in the fish, and lay the parcel on a baking sheet. Bake for 30 to 35 minutes until tender.

Remove the fish carefully from the foil and lay it on a warm dish. Discard the rosemary and the lemon slices from inside and pour over the anchovy sauce left in the foil. Serve at once with boiled potatoes to soak up the delicious juice.

Polpettone di Tonno _Tuna fish roll_

LIGURIA

In this recipe the tuna loses its strong tangy flavour and acquires a very delicate taste. Use good quality tuna, packed in oil. The _polpettone_ is an elegant dish, perfect for a buffet supper, a first course for a dinner party or a light meal for a summer day.

Preparation time: 20 minutes (plus 2 hours cooling)
Cooking time: 45 minutes
Serves: 4

200-g/7-oz can tuna, drained
2 whole eggs
1 hard-boiled egg, coarsely chopped
50 g/2 oz freshly grated Parmesan cheese
pinch of grated nutmeg
salt and freshly ground black pepper
100 ml/4 fl oz wine vinegar
100 ml/4 fl oz dry white wine
4–5 sprigs of fresh parsley
1 small onion, sliced
mayonnaise made with 1 egg yolk,
   150 ml/¼ pint olive oil, 30 ml/
   2 tablespoons lemon juice and a very
   little salt (see page 130)
30 ml/2 tablespoons olive oil
1·25 ml/¼ teaspoon lemon juice
black olives, lemon slices and capers to garnish

Flake and mash the tuna in a bowl. Add the eggs, the hard-boiled egg, the Parmesan, nutmeg and plenty of pepper. Mix thoroughly.

Moisten a piece of muslin, wring it out until just damp and lay it out flat. Place the tuna mixture on the cloth and roll it into a log shape, about 8 cm/3 inches in diameter. Wrap the muslin around it and tie both ends with string.

Place the roll with the vinegar, wine, parsley, onion and a little salt in an oval flameproof casserole, into which the roll will just fit. Add enough water to cover the roll by about 1 cm/½ inch. Cover and bring to the boil. Cook, over very low heat, for 45 minutes.

Remove the tuna roll and place it between two plates, put a weight on top and leave to cool for at least 2 hours.

While the tuna roll is cooling, make the mayonnaise.

When the roll is cold, unwrap it carefully and cut into 1 cm/½ inch slices. Arrange the slices, very slightly overlapping, on a dish. Mix together the olive oil and the lemon juice and spoon over the slices. Before serving, cover with the mayonnaise and garnish with black olives, lemon slices and capers.

Trance di Tonno in Agrodolce _Tuna fish steaks in sweet and sour sauce_

SICILY

The oiliness of the blue tuna fish combines deliciously with the sweet and sour flavour of the sauce. If frozen tuna is not available use filleted mackerels.

Preparation time: 10 minutes (plus 2 hours soaking)
Cooking time: 35 minutes
Serves: 4

4 tuna fish steaks, weighing about
   750 g/1½ lb
salt and freshly ground black pepper
75 ml/5 tablespoons wine vinegar,
   preferably red
45 ml/3 tablespoons olive oil
2 Spanish onions, cut into rings
30 ml/2 level tablespoons tomato purée,
   diluted in 225 ml/8 fl oz warm water
10 ml/2 level teaspoons sugar

Cover the fish steaks with cold water. Add 15 ml/1 level tablespoon salt and all but 30 ml/2 tablespoons of the vinegar. Leave for 2 hours.

Put the oil and the onions in a pan large enough to accommodate the fish in a single layer. Fry the onions until very soft and deep golden, stirring frequently.

Dry the fish thoroughly and add to the onions in the pan. Fry for 5 minutes, turning once. Add the diluted tomato purée, the remaining vinegar and the sugar, mix gently and cook, covered, over low heat for about 20 minutes, until the fish is tender, turning once.

Before serving, taste and adjust seasoning, adding some freshly ground black pepper, if you wish.

Burrida *Marinated Sardinian fish*

SARDINIA

Burrida, came to Sardinia from the Italian and French Rivieras. It is often served cold in the summer. Tuna, dogfish or skate are used in Sardinia, but any large white fish, such as haddock, is as good.

Preparation time: 30 minutes (plus 1 day marinating)
Cooking time: 20 minutes
Oven temperature: 200°C, 400°F, Gas Mark 6
Serves: 4

750 g/1½ lb fish fillets, cut into 5-cm/2-inch pieces
flour
vegetable oil
90 ml/6 tablespoons olive oil
2 garlic cloves, crushed
100 ml/4 fl oz wine vinegar
50 g/2 oz walnuts, finely chopped
50 g/2 oz pine nuts, finely chopped
30 ml/2 level tablespoons fresh dried breadcrumbs
1 small piece of fresh green chilli, seeded
2·5 ml/½ teaspoon grated nutmeg
salt and freshly ground black pepper

Wash and dry the fish and lightly coat with flour. Heat the vegetable oil in a heavy saucepan or deep fryer and deep fry the fish until pale golden. Drain on absorbent kitchen paper and set aside.

Put the olive oil and and garlic in a small saucepan and sauté for 30 seconds. Very slowly pour in the vinegar, taking care that the hot oil does not splash, then add 200 ml/7 fl oz of warm water. Boil for 5 minutes. Add the nuts, breadcrumbs, chilli, nutmeg and seasonings, mix well and cook for 10 minutes. Remove the chilli.

Put the fish in a dish and pour over the sauce. Cover and allow to marinate for a day in the refrigerator.

It can be eaten hot or cold. If you want to serve the dish hot, heat it, covered, in the oven for 20 minutes. If eating it cold, bring the dish to room temperature before serving.

Trance di Pesce al Cartoccio *Fish steaks baked in foil*

EMILIA-ROMAGNA

It has become very fashionable to cook food in foil or pastry in order to retain all its goodness. In Italy fish or chicken has been cooked in this way for a long time, using earthenware pots with tight-fitting lids, or strong greaseproof paper.

The best fish for this recipe is hake.

Preparation time: 40 minutes
Cooking time: 35 minutes
Oven temperature: 200°C, 400°F, Gas Mark 6
Serves: 4

8 mussels in their shells
4 fish steaks
100 g/4 oz prawns, peeled
2 large tomatoes, skinned, seeded and cut into thin strips
45 ml/3 tablespoons olive oil
30 ml/2 tablespoons dry white wine
30 ml/2 tablespoons chopped fresh parsley
salt and freshly ground black pepper

To clean the mussels, put them in a sink and scrub them thoroughly with a hard brush, scraping off any barnacles with a knife. Discard any mussels which are not tightly closed and put the rest in a colander under cold running water. Leave them for about 20 minutes.

When they are clean, place the mussels in a large saucepan. Cover and cook over high heat until the mussels are open, shaking the pan occasionally. Remove the mussel meat from the shells and discard the shells. Strain the cooking liquid through a sieve lined with muslin or with absorbent kitchen paper.

Cut 4 squares of aluminium foil, large enough to wrap a fish steak in. Grease the centres of the foil squares lightly with oil and on each place a fish steak. On top of each steak, put 2 mussels, and a quarter of the prawns and of the tomatoes.

In a bowl, mix together the oil, wine, the strained mussel liquid, parsley and salt and pepper, and pour some of this sauce over each fish steak. Wrap up each parcel by bringing the edges of the foil together at the top and twisting them. Place the parcels on a baking sheet or shallow ovenproof dish and bake in the oven for 35 minutes.

Serve the parcels on individual plates.

Trotelle al Vino Rosso

Trotelle al Vino Rosso   *Trout in red wine*

PIEDMONT

Don't be put off trying this because it breaches the well-established rule of white wine with fish. The red wine and anchovies give the trout a robust flavour.

Preparation time: 15 minutes
Cooking time: 30 minutes
Oven temperature: 200°C, 400°F,
  Gas Mark 6
Serves: 4

4 small trout, with heads and tails on
salt and freshly ground pepper
15 ml/1 tablespoon vegetable oil
1 celery stick, very finely chopped
2 shallots or 1 small onion, very finely
  chopped
1 carrot, very finely chopped
1 bouquet garni
300 ml/½ pint red wine
50 ml/2 fl oz fish stock or water
50 g/2 oz butter
15 ml/1 level tablespoon flour
5–10 ml/1–2 level teaspoons anchovy paste

Clean, wash and dry the trout. Lay them in a buttered ovenproof dish large enough to hold them in a single layer. Sprinkle with salt and pepper and cook in the oven for 10 minutes, turning them over after 5 minutes.

While the fish is cooking, put the oil and the chopped vegetables in a small saucepan and sweat the vegetables over very low heat for 10 minutes, stirring frequently.

Remove the dish from the oven and to it add the sweated vegetables, the bouquet garni, the wine and the fish stock. Return to the oven and cook for a further 15 minutes or until the trout are cooked.

Carefully lift the trout on to a heated serving dish and keep warm. Strain the cooking liquid into a small saucepan and bring to simmering point.

Blend together the butter, flour and anchovy paste and add, very gradually, to the simmering sauce, beating constantly.

To serve, pour half the sauce over the fish and serve the remaining sauce separately.

Pesce e Patate in Teglia *Baked fish and potatoes*

ABRUZZI-MOLISE

In Abruzzi the fish used for *Pesce e Patate in Teglia* is palombo. It is a long slim, shark-like fish which I have never seen in Britain, but I have been told that it is found in Devon where it is called Sweet William. Either monkfish or dogfish is a very satisfactory substitute.

Preparation time: 20 minutes
Cooking time: 50 minutes
Oven temperature: 180°C, 350°F,
 Gas Mark 4
Serves: 4

75 ml/3 fl oz olive oil
800 g/1¾ lb potatoes, cut into wafer-thin
 slices
1 onion, cut into thin rings
salt and freshly ground black pepper
1 small fresh chilli, seeded and chopped
30 ml/2 tablespoons chopped fresh parsley
1 garlic clove, finely chopped
550 g/1¼ lb fish steaks or fillets such as
 monkfish or dogfish

Grease a 25 × 20-cm/10 × 8-inch ovenproof dish with a little of the olive oil. Put half the potato slices and half the onion rings into the dish. Season and sprinkle with a little of the chilli, the parsley and half of the garlic.

Season the fish on both sides and lay it on the mixture. Pour over 45 ml/3 tablespoons of the oil, cover with the other half of the onion rings, then the potatoes and spoon over the remaining oil. Sprinkle with salt, pepper, and the remaining chilli and garlic.

Cover the dish with foil and bake in the oven for 30 minutes. Remove the foil and cook for a further 20 minutes, or until the potatoes are cooked. Serve from the baking dish.

Baccalà alla Trevisana *Salt cod cooked in milk and onions*

VENETO

Although I doubt whether salt cod will ever be popular in Britain, no Italian cookery book could ever be complete without giving at least one recipe out of the many in which it is used. In this one the salt cod is cooked in a similar way to smoked cod fillet, which it resembles in taste. Ask the fishmonger to cut the *baccalà* into 10 × 5-cm/4 × 2-inch pieces.

Preparation time: 30 minutes (plus 48 hours
 soaking)
Cooking time: 3 hours 20 minutes
Oven temperature: 170°C, 325°F,
 Gas Mark 3
Serves: 4

800 g/1¾ lb salt cod
100 g/4 oz flour
3 onions, sliced
salt and freshly ground black pepper
75 ml/3 fl oz vegetable oil
568 ml/1 pint milk
25 g/1 oz freshly grated Parmesan cheese
50 g/2 oz butter, diced

Soak the fish in cold water for 48 hours, changing the water at least 4 times during the soaking.

Put the fish under cold running water for 30 minutes. Skin it, remove all the bones, and dry thoroughly with absorbent kitchen paper. Coat the fish in the flour.

Grease a baking dish large enough to fit the fish in a single layer. Cover the bottom of the dish with half the onion, sprinkle with a little salt and plenty of pepper and pour over a few tablespoons of the oil. Cover with the fish, pour over more oil and finish with the remaining onion. Season with salt and pepper and pour over the milk and the rest of the oil. Cover the dish with foil and bake in the oven for 3 hours.

Remove from the oven, sprinkle with Parmesan and dot with the butter. Return the dish to the oven, uncovered, and cook for a further 20 minutes.

Serve piping hot with Polenta, (see page 110) as the Italians do, or with plain boiled potatoes.

Seppie alla Veneziana *Squid stewed in white wine*

VENETO

Squid is a most delicious fish. It is now available from many fishmongers and supermarkets, either imported or caught off the west coast of Britain. There are many ways of cooking squid but this Venetian recipe is a particular favourite of mine. Traditionally it would be accompanied by *polenta*, but plain boiled rice is equally good.

Preparation time: 45 minutes (plus 3 hours marinating)
Cooking time: 40 minutes
Serves: 4

1 kg/2 lb small squid, cleaned and 2 ink sacs reserved (see right)
75 ml/3 fl oz dry white wine
2 garlic cloves, crushed
30 ml/2 tablespoons olive oil
juice of ½ lemon
15 ml/1 tablespoon chopped fresh parsley

For the marinade:
50 ml/2 fl oz olive oil
salt and freshly ground black pepper

Cut the squid tentacles into 1-cm/½-inch strips. Put them into a bowl and pour over the marinade. Set aside for 3 hours.

Pour the squid and marinade into a large sauté pan and, when it is hot, cook the squid for 5 minutes, tossing frequently. Add the wine and garlic and cook for a further 5 minutes. Add the ink sacs, breaking them up with a spoon. Stir and check seasoning.

Cover the pan and cook over low heat for about 40 minutes, until the squid is pierced easily by a fork.

Add the remaining oil, the lemon juice and the parsley. Stir for about 3 minutes over high heat and serve piping hot.

To clean squid
Hold the body in one hand and with the other pull off the tentacles. As you do this, the contents of the body will come out too. Remove one or two of the dark little ink sacs, being very careful not to pierce them, and reserve them if they are needed in the recipe. Cut off the head and discard it; reserve the tentacles. Peel off the fine skin and pull out the backbone. Wash the squid thoroughly under cold water.

Seppie Ripiene *Stuffed squid*

MARCHE

These stuffed squid, stewed in red wine and olive oil, do not need to be accompanied by any vegetables, but should be followed by a French bean or a mixed salad.

Preparation time: 45 minutes
Cooking time: 1 hour
Oven temperature: 180°C, 350°F,
  Gas Mark 4
Serves: 4

4 large squid
60 ml/4 level tablespoons long-grain rice,
  cooked
30 ml/2 tablespoons vegetable oil
45 ml/3 tablespoons chopped fresh parsley
1 garlic clove, finely chopped
salt and freshly ground black pepper
30 ml/2 tablespoons red wine
30 ml/2 tablespoons olive oil

Clean the squid following the instructions on page 89. Wash the squid well, keeping the sacs whole.

Finely chop the squid tentacles, put into a bowl and add the rice, vegetable oil, parsley and garlic. Mix thoroughly. Season with salt and plenty of pepper.

Fill each sac with the rice and tentacle mixture. Do not pack the stuffing too tightly or the sac will burst during the cooking. Sew up the opening with thread. Lay the stuffed squid in a shallow ovenproof dish into which they will fit in a single layer. Mix together the wine and olive oil and pour over the squid. Bake in the oven, uncovered, for about 1 hour, until the squid can be easily pierced with a fork, basting every 15 minutes.

Cut the threads and pull them out before serving.

Sgombri alla Spezzina *Mackerels cooked in vinegar*

LIGURIA

Mackerel might not be the most elegant of fish, but it is certainly very tasty. Mackerels are plentiful in Britain during the winter and they are very economical. In this recipe the vinegar in which the fish is stewed cuts into the oiliness of the fish. This can also be served as an antipasto.

Preparation time: 10 minutes
Cooking time: 25 minutes
Serves: 4

3 medium or 2 large mackerels, filleted
2 onions, cut into rings
pinch of thyme
2 bay leaves, crumbled
salt and freshly ground pepper
200 ml/7 fl oz wine vinegar
100 ml/4 fl oz dry white wine

In a deep flameproof dish or sauté pan, place a layer of mackerel fillets and cover with a layer of onion rings, herbs, salt and pepper. Repeat until the ingredients are used up, ending with a layer of onion rings. Pour over the vinegar and the wine, bring slowly to the boil and simmer, covered, for about 20 minutes, until the fish is cooked but not broken up.

You can serve the fish either hot or cold with some of the cooking liquid spooned over.

Cefalo con le Zucchine *Grey mullet with courgettes*

MARCHE

Fish markets in any of the coastal towns on the Adriatic are a real joy to the eye. The stalls groan under the weight of fish, both familiar and unfamiliar, of which grey mullet is one of the most popular. It is a fish with a lovely flavour, but it must be eaten fresh. Its delicate taste is enhanced in this recipe by the inclusion of courgettes.

Preparation time: 20 minutes
Cooking time: 40 minutes
Oven temperature: 190°C, 375°F,
    Gas Mark 5
Serves: 4

500 g/1 lb courgettes, finely sliced
salt and freshly ground black pepper
15 ml/1 tablespoon chopped fresh parsley
1 garlic clove, finely chopped
one 1–1.25 kg/2–2½ lb fresh grey mullet,
    cleaned and gutted, with the head on
150 ml/¼ pint olive oil

Sprinkle the courgettes with salt and leave them to drain in a colander. Dry well with absorbent kitchen paper, place in a bowl, add the parsley and the garlic and mix thoroughly.

Season the fish with salt and a generous amount of pepper inside and out, and pour 15 ml/1 tablespoon of the oil inside. Lay the fish in a large ovenproof serving dish or roasting tin and spoon the courgettes and the remaining oil around it.

Cover with foil and bake in the oven for 20 minutes, basting after 10 minutes. Remove the foil, toss the courgettes and spoon some of the oil over the fish. Return the dish to the oven and cook for a further 20 minutes—basting after 10 minutes—until the flesh flakes easily.

Serve at once.

Cefalo con le Zucchine

Tortino di Sardine *Baked fresh sardines*

LIGURIA

When I first came to England, I used to long for this simple dish which reminded me of lovely holidays on the Riviera. But fresh sardines are never easily available in this country. Thanks to Alan Davidson's excellent book on Mediterranean fish, I discovered that sprats are of the same family as sardines and I find them a perfect substitute.

Preparation time: 30 minutes
Cooking time: 15 minutes
Oven temperature: 200°C, 400°F,
  Gas Mark 6
Serves: 4 as a first course

750 g/1½ lb fresh sardines or sprats
75 ml/5 level tablespoons fresh breadcrumbs
60 ml/4 tablespoons olive oil
30 ml/2 tablespoons wine vinegar
15 ml/1 level tablespoon capers
1 garlic clove, crushed
5 ml/1 teaspoon fresh marjoram
salt and freshly ground black pepper

Remove the heads and tails from the fish, open and gut them. Gently ease out the bones and discard. Wash the fish under cold running water and pat dry with absorbent kitchen paper.

In a bowl, combine the rest of the ingredients together.

Grease a shallow 20-cm/8-inch round ovenproof dish with oil and cover the bottom with a layer of the fish, arranged like the petals of a flower. Spread half the sauce evenly over it. Cover with another layer of fish and then the remaining sauce.

Bake in the oven for 15 minutes. Serve with Italian or crusty bread. The dish is equally good hot or cold.

Gamberi Imperiali in Tegame *King prawns stewed in wine*

LAZIO

The taste of the prawns is enhanced by cooking them in wine, which is briskly evaporated, thus concentrating the flavour. If you can, buy uncooked prawns, which are tastier, and peel them before cooking. Usually they are now sold pre-boiled and frozen, which is a great pity.

Preparation time: 10–15 minutes
Cooking time: 25 minutes
Serves: 4

90 ml/6 tablespoons olive oil
800 g/1¾ lb Dublin Bay prawns, peeled
30 ml/2 tablespoons brandy
100 ml/4 fl oz dry white wine
salt and freshly ground black pepper
5 ml/1 teaspoon lemon juice

Put the oil and prawns in a frying pan and sauté for about 5 minutes until golden, turning them over constantly. Add the brandy and wine, cover and cook for 10 to 15 minutes until tender. Uncover, add seasonings and boil rapidly until nearly all the liquid has evaporated. Add the lemon juice and serve at once.

VEGETABLES
AND SALADS

Rotolo di Spinaci   *Spinach roll*

LOMBARDY

I have always found that my mother's recipe for *Rotolo di Spinaci* with potato pasta is much nicer and easier than the traditional method, which uses home-made pasta. It is a very pretty green and cream roll and could be served as a first course at a dinner party.

Should you prefer it, instead of dressing it with melted butter and grated Parmesan, you could serve it covered with béchamel sauce (see page 133) and then browned in the oven.

Preparation time: 30 minutes
Cooking time: 45–50 minutes
Oven temperature: 200°C, 400°F,
  Gas Mark 6
Serves: 6

500 g/1 lb floury potatoes, such as
  King Edwards
1 onion, very finely chopped
15 ml/1 tablespoon vegetable oil
1 kg/2 lb spinach, cooked and chopped, or
  454-g/1-lb packet frozen chopped
  spinach, thawed and well drained
100 g/4 oz ricotta cheese
100 g/4 oz freshly grated Parmesan cheese
pinch of grated nutmeg
1 egg, plus 1 egg yolk
salt and freshly ground black pepper
5 ml/1 level teaspoon baking powder
about 200 g/7 oz flour
75 g/3 oz butter

Scrub the potatoes and boil them in their skins in plenty of slightly salted water for about 20 minutes, until tender.

While the potatoes are cooking, prepare the filling. Sauté the onion in the oil for 2 to 3 minutes until soft. Add the spinach and cook for a further 2 minutes, stirring frequently. Transfer the spinach to a bowl and add the ricotta, half the Parmesan, the nutmeg, egg yolk and salt and pepper. Mix very thoroughly.

When the potatoes are cooked, as soon as they are cool enough to handle, peel them and push through a sieve with the back of a wooden spoon straight on to a work surface. Make a well in the centre of the potatoes, drop the egg into it and add a little salt, the baking powder and most of the flour. Knead, adding more flour, if necessary, for about 5 minutes. The dough should be soft, smooth and slightly sticky. Shape the mixture into a ball.

Roll out the potato dough into a rectangle about 35·5 × 30·5 cm/14 × 12 inches. Spread the spinach filling over it evenly, leaving a 2-cm/¾-inch border all around. Roll the potato pastry into a sausage shape. Wrap the roll tightly in a muslin cloth and tie at each end.

Bring a large flameproof casserole of salted water to the boil and gently lower the roll into it. Return the water to the boil and simmer, partially covered, for 30 minutes. Unwrap and leave the roll to cool.

Cut the roll into 2-cm/¾-inch thick slices, and place them on a heated ovenproof dish, slightly overlapping. Melt the butter and pour it over the slices. Sprinkle with the remaining Parmesan. Bake in the oven for about 15 minutes, until golden.

Spinaci alla Romana   *Spinach in the Roman fashion*

LAZIO

This spinach is good with roast chicken, turkey or pork. It is often cooked in the same way in the Middle East where it is used as a filling for tiny savoury pastries.

Preparation time: 10 minutes
Cooking time: 10 minutes
Serves: 4

1 kg/2 lb fresh spinach
salt and freshly ground black pepper
25 g/1 oz sultanas
30 ml/2 tablespoons olive oil
50 g/2 oz butter
1 garlic clove, lightly crushed
25 g/1 oz pine nuts

Cook the spinach in a saucepan over moderate heat with a little salt and no water. Drain well and, when cool, squeeze out all the moisture with your hands. While the spinach is cooking, soak the sultanas in warm water for 10 minutes. Drain and dry on absorbent kitchen paper.

Sauté the oil, butter and the garlic clove in a frying pan for 1 minute. Discard the garlic and add the spinach, sultanas and pine nuts. Fry gently for 10 minutes, turning the mixture over frequently. Season with pepper and, if necessary, salt. Serve piping hot.

Rotolo di Spinaci

Fagiolini alla Fiorentina *French beans with fennel seeds*

TUSCANY

In Tuscany quite a few dishes are flavoured with fennel, which grows wild over the beautiful countryside. It is a lovely feathery herb which grows very well in this country too. If you have one in your garden use the leaves only for this dish; the flavour is milder than that of fennel seeds.

Preparation time: 20 minutes
Cooking time: 25 minutes
Serves: 4

500 g/1 lb French beans, topped and tailed
30 ml/2 tablespoons olive oil
30 ml/2 tablespoons vegetable oil
1 small onion, finely sliced
pinch of fennel seeds, pounded in a mortar
salt and freshly ground black pepper
350 g/12 oz tomatoes, skinned, seeded and
  chopped, or 227-g/8-oz can plum tomatoes,
  roughly chopped, with their juice

Part boil the beans in plenty of boiling salted water for 5 minutes. Drain.

Put the oils and the onion into a large pan and sauté for about 5 minutes, until the onion is soft and golden. Stir frequently, pressing the onion against the sides of the pan to release the juice. Add the fennel seeds, the beans and salt and pepper to taste and mix well. Stir in the tomatoes and simmer, covered, for 25 minutes, stirring occasionally.

Crespelle alla Fiorentina *Spinach-filled pancakes*

TUSCANY

Crespelle are thin pancakes stuffed, like *cannelloni*, with a variety of fillings. This is the Florentine version.

Preparation time: 50 minutes
Cooking time: 10 minutes
Oven temperature: 220°C, 425°F,
*   Gas Mark 7*
Serves: 4 as a main course

For the pancakes:
300 ml/½ pint milk
100 g/4 oz flour
2 eggs, beaten
pinch of salt
butter for frying

For the filling:
500 g/1 lb spinach or 226-g/8-oz packet
*   frozen chopped spinach, thawed*
50 g/2 oz butter
1 small onion, very finely chopped
75 g/3 oz freshly grated Parmesan cheese
pinch of grated nutmeg
béchamel sauce made with 568 ml/1 pint
*   milk, 50 g/2 oz butter and 50 g/2 oz flour*
*   (see page 133)*
salt and freshly ground black pepper

Pour the milk into a bowl and add the flour gradually, beating all the time, until the mixture is well blended. Then add the eggs and salt and beat again. Allow the mixture to stand for 30 minutes.

Make the filling while the batter is standing. Put the spinach in a pan without any water and cook over very low heat for 15 minutes. Frozen spinach needs only 5 minutes cooking. Squeeze all the water out with your hands and chop the spinach finely. Put the butter and the onion in a frying pan and sauté over medium heat until golden. Add the chopped spinach and cook for 2 to 3 minutes, stirring all the time. Transfer the mixture to a bowl. Add the grated Parmesan, nutmeg, 90 ml/6 tablespoons of béchamel, salt and pepper to taste and mix thoroughly.

To cook the pancakes, melt a knob of butter in a 18-cm/7-inch frying pan and then pour in enough batter (about 45 ml/3 tablespoons) to coat the base of the pan thinly. Over heat, rotate the pan very quickly to set the pancake. Cook both sides until pale brown and then transfer the pancake to a plate. Continue making pancakes, adding extra butter to the pan as required, until all the batter has been used. Pile the cooked pancakes on top of each other.

Lay the pancakes on a flat surface. Place an equal amount of the filling on each and spread it out, leaving a 1-cm/½-inch border around the edge. Roll up the pancakes loosely and place them with the folded-over edge underneath, in a single layer in a buttered ovenproof dish.

Pour over the remaining béchamel, making sure that all the pancakes are covered with the sauce. Dot with a little extra butter and place in the oven for about 10 minutes, until a golden crust has formed. Allow to settle for 5 minutes before serving.

Patate Mascé *Italian mashed potatoes*

EMILIA-ROMAGNA

The Italian version of mashed potatoes is certainly tastier than the British one and more robust than the classic French purée.

Preparation time: 15 minutes
Cooking time: 30 minutes
Serves: 4

1 kg/2 lb floury potatoes, such as King
*   Edwards*
salt and freshly ground black pepper
100 ml/4 fl oz milk
1 onion, sliced
1 garlic clove, very thinly sliced
50 g/2 oz butter
30 ml/2 tablespoons vegetable oil
30 ml/2 tablespoons freshly grated
*   Parmesan cheese*
15 ml/1 tablespoon chopped fresh parsley

Scrub the potatoes, put them in a saucepan with plenty of water and boil for about 20 minutes until tender. Add only a little salt, as this tends to make them burst. Drain them and, as soon as they are cool enough to handle, remove the skins. Put the potatoes through a food-mill, or push through a sieve using the back of a wooden spoon. Season and mix well.

Pour the milk into a saucepan and heat gently. In another, larger, saucepan sauté the onion and garlic in the butter and oil until slightly coloured. Add the potato purée and turn it over and over to absorb all the fat. Slowly add enough hot milk, mixing constantly, to make a rather stiff purée. Mix in the cheese and the parsley. Taste and adjust the seasonings.

Caponatina *Aubergines in a sweet and sour sauce*

SICILY

This is one of the glories of the Sicilian kitchen. It is eaten in every town on the island, sometimes with the addition of sultanas and pine nuts, or served with tuna. Use first-class vegetables and the best olive oil you can afford.

*Preparation time: 10 minutes (plus
    30 minutes draining)*
Cooking time: 35 minutes
Serves: 4

*750 g/1½ lb aubergines, cut into 2·5-cm/
    1-inch cubes*
salt and freshly ground black pepper
vegetable oil
*the inner sticks of 1 small celery head,
    coarse threads removed, and cut into
    3·5-cm/1½-inch long matchsticks*
75 ml/3 fl oz olive oil
1 onion, sliced
226-g/8-oz can plum tomatoes, drained
15 ml/1 level tablespoon granulated sugar
100 ml/4 fl oz red wine vinegar
50 g/2 oz capers
*50 g/2 oz large green olives, stoned and
    quartered*

Sprinkle the aubergine cubes with salt and place them in a colander to drain. Put a weight on top. Leave them to stand for at least 30 minutes, then dry them well on absorbent kitchen paper.

Heat 2·5 cm/1 inch of vegetable oil in a frying pan. When the oil is hot, add a layer of aubergines and fry until golden brown on all sides. Drain them on absorbent kitchen paper. Repeat until all the aubergines are cooked.

Dry the celery and fry it in the same oil as the aubergines, until golden and crisp. Drain them on absorbent kitchen paper.

Pour the olive oil into a clean frying pan and add the onion. Cook gently for about 3 minutes until soft and just coloured. Put the tomatoes through the fine holes of a food-mill and add to the onion with the sugar, salt and pepper and cook, stirring frequently, over moderately high heat for 15 minutes. Then add the vinegar, capers, olives, aubergines and celery and cook, over very low heat, for a further 15 minutes. Taste and adjust the seasonings.

Pour the caponatina into a serving dish and allow to cool. Serve at room temperature.

Tortino di Zucchine *Courgettes baked with breadcrumbs*

EMILIA-ROMAGNA

Courgettes are one of the most popular vegetables in Italy. Now they are available here practically the whole year round. You should buy bright coloured, small, firm courgettes with glossy, smooth skin.

Preparation time: 35 minutes
Cooking time: 10–15 minutes
*Oven temperature: 220°C, 425°F,
    Gas Mark 7*
Serves: 6

25 g/1 oz butter
45 ml/3 tablespoons vegetable oil
1 kg/2 lb courgettes, cut into thin rounds
salt and freshly ground black pepper
*béchamel sauce made with 1 litre/1¾ pints
    milk, 75 g/3 oz butter and 75 g/3 oz flour
    (see page 133)*
2 egg yolks
*45 ml/3 tablespoons freshly grated
    Parmesan cheese*
2·5 ml/½ teaspoon of grated nutmeg

Put the butter and oil in a large frying pan and, when hot, sauté the courgettes for 15 minutes, stirring occasionally. Add salt and pepper.

Meanwhile, prepare the béchamel sauce following the instructions on page 133. When cooked, remove from the heat, cool a little and then mix in the egg yolks and the Parmesan. Add the nutmeg and salt and pepper to taste.

Turn the courgettes into a buttered large shallow ovenproof dish and cover with the cheese sauce. Bake for 10 to 15 minutes until a golden crust has formed. Allow the dish to settle for 5 minutes before serving.

Torta Pasqualina   *Spinach pie from Genoa*

LIGURIA

Pasqua means Easter in Italian. This pie is served on Easter Sunday in Genoa, where it is made with Swiss chard or small artichokes. This recipe uses spinach as both Swiss chard and small artichokes are hard to find here in Britain.

Preparation time: 40 minutes
Cooking time: 1 hour
Oven temperature: 200°C, 400°F,
  Gas Mark 6
Serves: 6

1 kg/2 lb spinach, cooked, or 500 g/1 lb
  frozen leaf spinach, thawed
1 small onion, finely chopped
75 ml/5 tablespoons olive oil
7 eggs
salt and freshly ground black pepper
400 g/14 oz ricotta cheese
150 ml/¼ pint single cream
75 g/3 oz freshly grated Parmesan cheese
15 ml/1 level tablespoon flour
454-g/1-lb packet of frozen puff pastry,
  thawed
15 g/½ oz butter
15 ml/1 tablespoon chopped fresh marjoram

Squeeze all the water out of the spinach and chop coarsely. In a frying pan, sauté the onion in 45 ml/3 tablespoons of the oil for 1 minute, add the spinach and cook for a further 1 minute. Transfer the spinach mixture into a bowl and when cool, beat in 1 egg. Add salt and pepper to taste and set aside.

Sieve the ricotta into a bowl, beat in the cream and add 50 g/2 oz of the Parmesan.

Grease a 21-cm/8½-inch round cake tin, sprinkle with flour and shake out any excess. Roll out two-thirds of the pastry and use to line the base and sides of the tin. Brush with 15 ml/1 tablespoon olive oil, cover the base with the ricotta mixture and then with the spinach. Trim the pastry sides to 0·5 cm/¼ inch above the filling. Reserve the trimmings.

Make 6 large hollows in the spinach, put a knob of butter into each and then drop in an egg. Sprinkle each egg with some marjoram, Parmesan cheese and a little seasoning.

Roll out the remaining pastry to a 21·5 cm/8½ inch round. Dampen the edges and use the pastry round to cover the top of the pie. Seal the edges and pierce the top in several places with a fork. Use the reserved pastry timmings to decorate and brush with the remaining oil. Bake in the oven for about 1 hour, until golden brown, covering the top with foil, if necessary, to prevent over-browning.

Serve at once.

Patate col Diavolicchio   *Potatoes with chilli and oil*

BASILICATA

Avoid floury potatoes when you are making this dish. If you are fond of chillies you can add more.

Preparation time: 10 minutes
Cooking time: 30 minutes
Serves: 6

1 kg/2 lb red-skinned potatoes such as
  Desirée
salt
75 ml/5 tablespoons olive oil
2·5-cm/1-inch piece of fresh chilli, seeded
  and very finely chopped
2 garlic cloves, finely chopped

Cook the potatoes in their skins in boiling salted water until just tender. Drain and peel as soon as they are cool enough to handle. Cool slightly, then cut into slices and sprinkle with salt.

Heat the oil in a pan. Add the chilli and garlic and fry for about 3 minutes until the garlic is lightly coloured. Take care not to burn the garlic or it will have a bitter taste. Pour the mixture over the potatoes. Toss gently together and serve warm.

Torta Pasqualina

Pasticcio di Patate *Baked purée of potatoes*

UMBRIA

This dish can be prepared in advance and baked just before serving. The mortadella gives it a special spicy taste, sharpened by the lemon rind.

Preparation time: 35 minutes
Cooking time: 20 minutes
Oven temperature: 190°C, 375°F,
   Gas Mark 5
Serves: 6

1·5 kg/3 lb floury potatoes, such as King
   Edwards
90 ml/6 tablespoons milk
50 g/2 oz butter
2 eggs
15 ml/1 tablespoon freshly grated
   Parmesan cheese
7–8 basil leaves, coarsely chopped, or
   15 ml/1 tablespoon chopped fresh parsley
salt and freshly ground black pepper
1·25 ml/¼ teaspoon grated lemon rind
pinch of grated nutmeg
100 g/4 oz mortadella, cut into very small
   squares
50 g/2 oz mozzarella or Bel Paese cheese,
   cut into very small cubes
45 ml/3 level tablespoons fresh dried
   breadcrumbs

In a large saucepan, boil the potatoes in their skins in plenty of lightly salted water until tender. Drain and peel as soon as they are cool enough to handle. Purée the potatoes through a food-mill and then beat in the milk and 40 g/1½ oz of the butter. Set aside.

Mix together the eggs, the Parmesan and the basil or parsley in a bowl. Season with salt and pepper, lemon rind and nutmeg. Add the egg mixture to the potato purée, mix well and then stir in the mortadella and the cheese.

Butter a 1·4-litre/2½-pint soufflé dish and sprinkle with 30 ml/2 tablespoons of breadcrumbs. Shake off any excess crumbs. Spoon the potato mixture into the dish, smooth the top with a palette knife, sprinkle with remaining breadcrumbs and dot with the remaining butter. Bake in the oven for about 20 minutes until golden. Allow to settle for 5 minutes before serving.

Funghi Trifolati *Sautéed mushrooms with parsley and garlic*

LIGURIA

You can cook courgettes or aubergines (previously salted and sweated) in the same way as these mushrooms, which can be served hot with grilled meat or fish, or at room temperature as an antipasto.

Preparation time: 10 minutes
Cooking time: 10 minutes
Serves: 4

2 garlic cloves, finely chopped
90 ml/6 tablespoons olive oil
500 g/1 lb firm white mushrooms,
   cut into 0·5-cm/¼-inch slices
salt and freshly ground black pepper
30 ml/2 tablespoons chopped fresh parsley

In a heavy frying pan, sauté the garlic in the oil over moderate heat for 1 to 2 minutes until lightly coloured. Turn the heat up to high, add the mushrooms and stir until they have absorbed the oil. Reduce the heat to low, add the seasonings and mix well. When the juice has come out of the mushrooms, turn the heat up and cook for 4 to 5 minutes, stirring frequently.

Sprinkle with parsley, stir again and serve.

Insalata di Finocchi e Ricotta *Fennel and ricotta salad*

TUSCANY

A delicious salad which can be served after the main course or as antipasto.

Preparation time: 10 minutes
Serves: 4

2 fennel bulbs, cut into thin strips
200 g/7 oz ricotta cheese
60 ml/4 tablespoons olive oil
5 ml/1 teaspoon lemon juice
salt and freshly ground black pepper

Put the fennel in a salad bowl and crumble the ricotta on to it. Dress with the oil, lemon juice, salt and pepper and toss well.

Peperoni Arrostiti con Filetti di Acciughe e Uova Sode *Charred peppers with anchovy fillets and hard-boiled eggs*

CALABRIA

Peeling the peppers for this salad takes a little time but the result is worth the effort.

Preparation time: 30 minutes (plus 30 minutes standing)
Serves: 4

4 large yellow peppers
1 garlic clove
salt and freshly ground black pepper
60 ml/4 tablespoons olive oil
30 ml/2 tablespoons chopped fresh parsley
4 eggs, hard-boiled and cut in half
50-g/2-oz can anchovy fillets, drained

Place the peppers under a preheated grill or on a wire rack directly over a gas flame. Cook, turning, until the skin is black and charred all over. Peel off the burnt skin, using a small knife. Wipe the peppers with absorbent kitchen paper. Cut each pepper into quarters, remove and discard the seeds and white ribs and cut into thin strips.

Put the garlic on a wooden board, cover with 5 ml/1 level teaspoon salt and crush it with the blade of a knife. Scrape the garlic and salt into a bowl and add the oil, parsley and seasonings. Mix well together.

Arrange the eggs, strips of peppers and anchovy fillets on a dish and spoon over the sauce. Allow to stand for at least 30 minutes before serving.

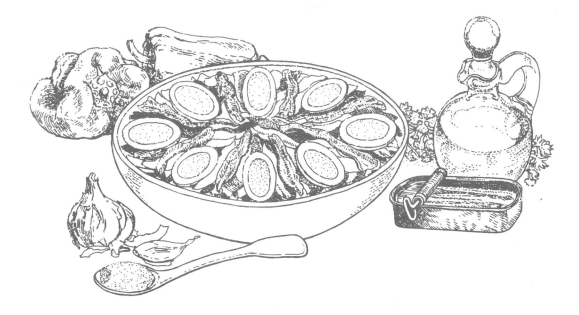

From the left, clockwise: Finocchi al Latte, Broccoli 'Strascinati' in Padella and Cipolline in Agrodolce

Broccoli 'Strascinati' in Padella *Sautéed broccoli with oil and garlic*

LAZIO

A favourite way of cooking broccoli. Jane Grigson, in her *Vegetable Book*, suggests that cauliflower is also good sautéed in this fashion.

Preparation time: 10 minutes
Cooking time: 15 minutes
Serves: 4

750 g/1½ lb broccoli
45 ml/3 tablespoons olive oil
2 garlic cloves, finely sliced
1 fresh chilli
salt

Wash the broccoli and separate the florets from the stems and leaves. You can use the stems and leaves at another meal, boiled and tossed in butter.

In a frying pan large enough to hold the broccoli in a single layer, heat the oil, garlic and the whole chilli. When the garlic is just coloured, discard the chilli and add the broccoli. Add the salt, toss the broccoli well in the oil, cover the pan and cook, over very low heat, for 12 to 15 minutes until tender. Stir frequently during the cooking and, if the broccoli become too dry, add a few tablespoons of warm water.

102

Finocchi al Latte   *Fennel with milk and cheese*

UMBRIA

Fennel is now easily available in Britain and is usually very good. It goes very well with roast or grilled meats or with *Frittata* (see page 56).

Preparation time: 10 minutes
Cooking time: 12 minutes
Serves: 4

2 large fennel bulbs, each weighing about
    350–400 g/12–14 oz or 3 small ones,
    trimmed of all foliage and cut in half
salt
25 g/1 oz butter
75 ml/5 tablespoons milk
45 ml/3 tablespoons freshly grated
    Parmesan cheese

Slice the fennel horizontally. Wash and dry with absorbent kitchen paper.

Bring a large saucepan of salted water to the boil and cook the fennel for 5 to 7 minutes until tender. Drain.

Melt the butter in a frying pan, add the fennel and cook very gently for 1 minute on each side, until soft but not coloured. Add the milk, cook gently for 5 minutes, stirring frequently, and then transfer to an ovenproof dish. Sprinkle with the Parmesan and place under a hot grill for 2 minutes for the cheese to brown.

Cipolline in Agrodolce   *Sweet and sour onions*

EMILIA-ROMAGNA

This dish should be made with small white onions which, unfortunately, are not easily available in Britain. If you cannot buy them, use pickling onions and add a little more sugar. They are delicious with cold meats.

Preparation time: 15 minutes
Cooking time: 1½ hours
Serves: 4

750 g/1½ lb small white onions
50 g/2 oz butter, cut into small pieces
325 ml/11 fl oz water
15 ml/1 level tablespoon tomato purée,
    diluted in 30 ml/2 tablespoons warm
    water
15 ml/1 level tablespoon sugar
30 ml/2 tablespoons wine vinegar
salt and freshly ground black pepper

Plunge the onions into boiling water for a few seconds, and then skin them. If you are using pickling onions, soak them in cold water for 30 minutes, then skin. Do not remove the root, or the onions will break during the cooking.

Put the onions into a frying pan in a single layer and add the butter, water and diluted tomato purée. Cook, uncovered, over moderate heat for 30 minutes, stirring frequently. Add more water if necessary, during the cooking.

Add the sugar, vinegar and the seasonings. Mix well, turn the heat down to low, and continue cooking, uncovered, for about 1¼ hours, adding more water, if necessary. The onions are ready when they are a rich brown colour and can easily be pierced by a fork.

Serve either hot or cold.

Panzanella *Bread salad*

TUSCANY

In Tuscany this bread salad is made with the local bread, two days old. The bread is soaked in water, squeezed, and added to the rest of the salad. The result is excellent, but Tuscan bread is different from the bread we can buy here, and I have never been successful with this dish. That is until I tried this version of *Panzanella*, based on the one Marcella Hazan gives in *The Classic Italian Cookbook*, which is made with fried croûtons.

Preparation time: 20 minutes
Serves: 4

vegetable oil
4 slices good quality white bread, crustless
 and cut into 2·5-cm/1-inch squares
8 anchovy fillets
1 small garlic clove, finely sliced
30 ml/2 tablespoons chopped fresh parsley
7–8 basil leaves, chopped or 10 ml/2
 teaspoons fresh chopped oregano
15 ml/1 level tablespoon capers
75 ml/3 fl oz olive oil
30 ml/2 tablespoons wine vinegar
salt and freshly ground black pepper
2 red onions, very finely sliced
500 g/1 lb tomatoes, skinned and cut into
 chunks
6 black olives
1 egg, hard-boiled and cut into wedges

Heat enough oil in a frying pan to come 1 cm/½ inch up the sides of the pan. When hot, slide in enough bread cubes to fit in a single layer, turn the heat down a little and fry until light golden. Drain the bread on absorbent kitchen paper. Repeat until all the bread has been fried.

Meanwhile finely chop 6 anchovy fillets and put them in a bowl with the garlic, parsley, basil or oregano and capers. Add olive oil and vinegar, salt and plenty of pepper and stir thoroughly. Add the croûtons, the onions, and the tomatoes and toss well. Level the top of the panzanella and decorate with the remaining anchovy fillets, the olives and the pieces of egg. Cover with cling film and refrigerate for 1 hour before serving.

The croûtons can be made in advance, but not more than 12 hours before serving them.

Carote al Marsala *Carrots braised in Marsala*

SICILY

In Sicily these carrots are usually prepared without cream, but I mix in two tablespoons two minutes before serving and this makes them even more delicious.

Preparation time: 10 minutes
Cooking time: 30 minutes
Serves: 4

50 g/2 oz butter
750 g/1½ lb carrots, thinly sliced
salt
100 ml/4 fl oz Marsala or sweet sherry
30 ml/2 tablespoons home-made meat stock
 (see page 138)

Heat the butter in a pan and when the foam begins to subside, add the carrots. Toss them over thoroughly in the butter, add salt and then pour over the Marsala. Cook for 10 minutes then add the stock. Stir well, cover the pan and cook over low heat for about 20 minutes, until tender.

Carote in Insalata   *Grated carrots with olive oil and lemon juice*

SOUTHERN ITALY

You can serve these carrots either as a simple antipasto or as an accompaniment to grilled or cold meat.

Preparation time: 10 minutes
Serves: 4

250 g/9 oz young carrots, grated
heart of 1 celery head, cut into fine strips
60 ml/4 tablespoons olive oil
15 ml/1 tablespoon lemon juice
5 ml/1 level teaspoon sugar
salt and freshly ground black pepper

Put the grated carrots and celery strips into a salad bowl. Combine the rest of the ingredients in a bowl, mix thoroughly and pour over the salad. Toss well and serve at once.

Croquettes di Patate al Forno   *Baked potato cakes*

LOMBARDY

As much as I love fried food, I find the difficulty with it is that it must be eaten straight away. For this reason, instead of frying these croquettes, which is the more traditional way, I prefer to bake them as they do in Bergamo, in north-east Lombardy. Croquettes prepared in this way are equally delicious and certainly less fattening.

Preparation time: 10 minutes
Cooking time: 40 minutes
Oven temperature: 230°C, 450°F,
  Gas Mark 8
Serves: 4

750 g/1½ lb floury potatoes, such as King
  Edwards
150 g/5 oz butter
1 egg
45 ml/3 tablespoons freshly grated
  Parmesan cheese
salt and freshly ground black pepper

Scrub the potatoes and boil them in their skins in a large saucepan of water (add very little salt to the water) for about 20 minutes. Peel the potatoes as soon as they are cool enough to handle, and then purée them. Add 100 g/4 oz of the butter, cut into small pieces. Fold in the egg, the cheese and seasonings and mix well.

Butter a baking sheet. Form the potato mixture into about 16 balls the size of a small egg—wet your hands from time to time to prevent the mixture sticking. Place the balls on the baking sheet. Melt the remaining butter and brush each ball generously with it.

Bake in the oven for about 20 minutes until the potato cakes are golden.

Leave to settle for 5 minutes before serving. If they are too hot you will not be able to taste the Parmesan cheese.

Cavolfiore Lesso in Insalata *Boiled cauliflower salad*

NORTHERN ITALY

Many salads in Italy are made with lightly boiled vegetables. Courgettes, French beans or spinach are extremely good treated in this way. You can vary the dressing by adding black olives or chopped anchovy fillets.

Preparation time: 5 minutes
Cooking time: 10–15 minutes
Serves: 4–6

1 cauliflower, weighing about 1 kg/2 lb,
    trimmed
60 ml/4 tablespoons olive oil
lemon juice to taste
salt and freshly ground black pepper
1 egg, hard-boiled

Boil the cauliflower in plenty of salted water for 10 to 15 minutes, until tender but firm. Drain immediately.

Meanwhile whisk the oil, lemon juice, salt and pepper together.

Detach the florets from the head, dividing the bigger ones in two or three parts. Put them in a bowl and pour over the dressing. The cauliflower will need a generous amount. Toss very carefully.

Purée the hard-boiled egg through the finest holes of a food-mill directly onto the cauliflower.

Serve at room temperature.

Peperonata *Ratatouille of yellow and red peppers*

PUGLIA

A dish cooked in a similar way to the French *Ratatouille*, but using only peppers and tomatoes. Like *Ratatouille* its flavour improves if it is cooled and left to stand for a while. It is delicious cold as an antipasto, or hot as an accompaniment to boiled, roast or grilled meat. If you have any left, use it to dress some spaghetti, adding to it 30 ml/2 tablespoons of olive oil.

Preparation time: 15 minutes
Cooking time: 30 minutes
Serves: 4

75 ml/3 fl oz olive oil
500 g/1 lb red and yellow peppers, seeded
    and cut into thin strips
15 ml/1 tablespoon chopped fresh parsley
1 garlic clove, finely chopped
397-g/14-oz can plum tomatoes, with their
    juice
salt and freshly ground black pepper

Heat the oil in a large frying pan and cook the peppers gently for 2 to 3 minutes, stirring frequently. Add the parsley and the garlic and cook for a further 1 minute. Coarsely chop the tomatoes and add them and their juice to the pan. Stir and add seasoning.

Cover the pan and cook over low heat for about 30 minutes, until the peppers are tender. The sauce should be quite thick. If necessary, uncover the pan and boil the peperonata rapidly to reduce.

Cavolfiore Lesso in Insalata and, below, Peperonata

Scarpazza   *Spinach cake*

LOMBARDY

Quite a few dishes from Lombardy mix together sweet and savoury ingredients, which gives to the cooking of this region a highly sophisticated taste. Nowadays this spinach cake is served as a first course, or a second course in a light supper, but in days gone by it was often served as a pudding, in which case some sugar replaced the salt and pepper and the Parmesan.

Preparation time: 30 minutes
Cooking time: 1 hour
Oven temperature: 200°C, 400°F,
   Gas Mark 6
Serves: 6

50 g/2 oz stale white bread, crustless
568 ml/1 pint milk
115 g/4½ oz butter
40 g/1½ oz flour
1 kg/2 lb spinach, cooked, or 500 g/lb
   frozen spinach, thawed
3 eggs
25 g/1 oz almonds, blanched and chopped
25 g/1 oz pine nuts
25 g/1 oz digestive biscuits, crushed
25 g/1 oz sultanas
1·25 ml/¼ level teaspoon fennel seeds
2·5 ml/½ level teaspoon ground cinnamon
30 ml/2 tablespoons freshly grated
   Parmesan cheese
salt and freshly ground black pepper

Put the bread in a bowl, cover with the milk and leave for 30 minutes. Then break it up with a fork and beat to a paste.

Meanwhile melt 100 g/4 oz of the butter in a saucepan, add the flour and cook for 2 minutes, stirring constantly. Add the bread and milk mixture and cook over very low heat for 5 minutes.

Meanwhile, after squeezing all the water out of it with your hands, add the spinach to the saucepan. Cook for 1 minute, stirring all the time. Remove from the heat, pour the mixture into a bowl and allow to cool a little.

Beat the eggs lightly together and stir them into the spinach mixture. Add all the remaining ingredients. Taste and adjust the seasonings.

Butter a 24-cm/9½-inch cake tin and line with foil. Grease the foil with oil. Spoon the mixture into the tin and dot with the remaining butter. Cover with foil and bake in the oven for 20 minutes. Remove the foil and bake for a further 40 minutes, or until a skewer inserted into the middle of the cake comes out dry. Allow to cool.

Remove from the tin and serve at room temperature. If you wish, you can accompany it with a plain tomato sauce (see page 132).

RICE,
POLENTA AND
GNOCCHI

Polenta *Cornmeal pudding*

Polenta is a very digestible, nourishing and versatile food much eaten in northern Italy. In the mountains of Piedmont, it is a staple food, served with butter and local cheeses, or as an accompaniment to rich stews, or even as a dessert.

Although *Polenta* is very easily made, it does need care and patience. Choose a deep and heavy saucepan and mix with a long wooden spoon, because sometimes, while cooking, it can splatter over your hand.

Buy coarse-grained cornmeal and avoid buying pre-cooked *Polenta*, which I think is not good, even if it saves some stirring.

Cooking time: 30 minutes
Serves: 6 as an accompaniment

300 g/11 oz coarse-grain cornmeal or
polenta flour
10 ml/2 level teaspoons salt
vegetable oil

Bring 1·5 litres/2½ pints salted water to simmering point and add the cornmeal in a very thin stream. (The easiest way is to pick up a handful of cornmeal and let it run through your semi-closed fingers.) Stir vigorously to avoid forming lumps. Simmer steadily for 20 to 30 minutes, stirring frequently, until the polenta comes easily off the sides of the pan. Turn on to a round wooden board and spread with a wooden spoon into a dome-shape about 12·5 cm/5 inches high, or turn into a warm serving dish.

Serve hot.

Fried polenta
Turn the polenta on to a wooden board as above. Spread into a cake shape about 5 cm/2 inches high and leave to cool.

When cold, divide the polenta into four sections and then cut each section into 1-cm/½-inch thick slices. Heat enough vegetable oil in a frying pan to come 2 cm/¾ inch up the sides of the pan. When the oil is very hot, cook the polenta slices, several at a time, for about 3 minutes on each side until the outside is crisp. Drain on absorbent kitchen paper.

Serve at once.

Polenta

Risotto alla Milanese
Risotto with beef marrow and saffron

LOMBARDY

Strongly reminiscent of *Paella*, this beautiful pale golden risotto is coloured with saffron, which also gives it its distinctive flavour. The use of saffron came from the Arabs via Spain during the centuries of the Spanish occupation of Lombardy. In Italy risotto is served by itself, as a first course.

Preparation time: 5 minutes
Cooking time: 35 minutes
Serves: 4

1 litre/1¾ pints meat stock (see page 138)
1 shallot or 1 small onion, finely chopped
50 g/2 oz beef marrow or pancetta, finely
    chopped
75 g/3 oz butter
350 g/12 oz arborio or other Italian rice
75 ml/3 fl oz dry white wine
pinch of saffron
salt, if necessary, and freshly ground black
    pepper
50 g/2 oz freshly grated Parmesan cheese

Bring the stock to simmering point and keep it at a slow, steady simmer.

Meanwhile, in a large frying pan sauté the shallot and the beef marrow gently in 50 g/2 oz of the butter until translucent. Add the rice to the pan and stir it until well coated with butter. Pour in the wine and 200 ml/7 fl oz of the simmering stock. Stirring constantly, cook over moderate heat until the liquid has been absorbed, then add another 150 ml/¼ pint of the stock. The risotto should remain at simmering point during the cooking. Keep stirring and adding more stock, a little at a time, never letting the rice dry out. You might not need to use the quantity of stock given here—the risotto should be creamy, not runny. It is ready when the rice is *al dente*, firm to the bite.

About half-way through cooking time—the risotto will take about 25 minutes—add the saffron and the pepper. Taste and, if necessary, add salt.

When cooked, turn off the heat, add the remaining butter and 30 ml/2 tablespoons of the cheese. Stir well and transfer the risotto to a warm dish. Serve immediately with the remaining Parmesan in a bowl.

Risotto con gli Spinaci
Risotto with spinach

ABRUZZI-MOLISE

I was recently in Rome and had some outstanding meals at 'La Maiella', a restaurant owned by Signor Antonio. I always eat what he suggests and he never lets me down. This is his recipe.

Preparation time: 20 minutes
Cooking time: 25–30 minutes
Serves: 4

500 g/1 lb spinach, cooked, or 226-g/8-oz
    packet frozen leaf spinach, thawed
75 g/3 oz butter
15 ml/1 tablespoon vegetable oil
1 small onion, finely chopped
300 g/11 oz arborio or other Italian rice
75 ml/5 tablespoons dry white wine
1 litre/1¾ pints hot chicken stock or 2
    chicken stock cubes dissolved in the same
    quantity of boiling water
salt and freshly ground black pepper
30 ml/2 tablespoons double cream
30 ml/2 tablespoons freshly grated
    Parmesan cheese

Squeeze all the water out of the spinach and chop it finely. Heat the butter and oil in a large heavy saucepan. Add the onion and sauté until translucent. Put in the spinach and cook for 2 minutes, then add the rice and mix thoroughly over heat for a further 1 minute. Pour over the wine, boil briskly for 1 minute and then add about a third of the hot stock.

Stirring constantly, cook over moderate heat until the liquid has been absorbed, then add another third of the stock. The risotto should remain at simmering point during the cooking. Keep stirring and adding more stock, a little at a time, never letting the rice dry out. You might not need to use the quantity of stock given here—the risotto should be creamy, not runny. It is ready when the rice is *al dente*, firm to the bite. It will cook in about 25 minutes, but the time will vary according to the kind of rice you use.

Season with salt and pepper. Add the cream and stir vigorously. Remove from the heat and add the Parmesan. Stir again before transferring to a warm serving dish. Serve at once.

Polenta Pasticciata   *Baked polenta with meat and mushroom sauce*

VENETO

In Italian homes *Polenta* is usually made in large quantities, one half eaten on the same day, the other used a day or two later in different ways: sometimes fried with *Fegato alla Veneziana* (see page 65) or with *Fagiano alla Milanese* (see page 79) or baked with meat sauce or with béchamel sauce and cheese.

Preparation time: 45 minutes
Cooking time: 1½ hours
Oven temperature: 200°C, 400°F,
  Gas Mark 6
Serves: 6

polenta (see page 110)
50 g/2 oz pancetta or unsmoked streaky
  bacon, cut into fine strips
45 ml/3 tablespoons vegetable oil
1 onion, finely chopped
1 celery stick, finely chopped
1 carrot, finely chopped
225 g/8 oz luganega or other coarse-grained,
  mild Continental sausage, skinned
225 g/8 oz chuck steak, cut into very
  small pieces
45 ml/3 tablespoons dry white wine
397-g/14-oz can plum tomatoes, with their
  juice
salt and freshly ground black pepper
75 g/3 oz butter
1 garlic clove, lightly crushed
225 g/8 oz mushrooms, sliced
100 g/4 oz fresh chicken livers, cut into
  small pieces
50 g/2 oz freshly grated Parmesan cheese

Make the polenta following the instructions on page 110. Pour the polenta on to a wooden board or cold surface and spread into a cake shape about 5 cm/2 inches thick. Leave to cool.

Meanwhile fry the pancetta in the oil for 2 minutes. Add the onion, celery and carrot and continue frying until soft. Add the sausage and sauté for 2 minutes, breaking up the sausage with a fork, and then add the steak and brown well. Pour over the wine, raise the heat and boil until it has nearly evaporated. Add the tomatoes and their juice and the seasonings. Stir, cover the saucepan and simmer for 1 hour until the meat is tender. If the sauce gets too dry during the cooking, add a little warm water or stock.

To make the mushroom sauce, put 50 g/2 oz of the butter and the whole garlic clove into a frying pan over low heat. When the butter foam begins to subside, add the mushrooms and sauté for 5 minutes. Discard the garlic, add the chicken livers and cook for 2 minutes, stirring frequently. Taste and adjust seasoning.

Cut the polenta into 4 sections and then into 1-cm/½-inch thick slices.

Butter a deep ovenproof dish and cover the bottom with a layer of polenta slices. Spread half the meat sauce over it, then spread with a third of the mushroom sauce and sprinkle with half the Parmesan. Repeat this layering and then finish with a layer of polenta and mushroom sauce. Sprinkle with the remaining Parmesan and dot with the remaining butter.

Bake in the oven for 15 to 20 minutes until a light crust is formed. Remove the dish from the oven and allow to settle for 5 minutes before serving.

Risi e Bisi *Rice and peas*

VENETO

The Venetians are masters of the art of cooking rice and this is the most celebrated of their rice dishes. Indeed it is the aristocrat of all rice dishes; it was served at the Doge's banquet each year on St Mark's feast day (which falls on 25th April when the first young peas are just coming in!). It resembles very thick soup or thin risotto. Some restaurants in Venice provide a fork, as well as a spoon, to eat it with. But it is best when fairly runny.

Purists say that true *Risi e Bisi* can only be prepared in Venice, because the peas must come from the vegetable gardens of the lagoon. But I think it is delicious even when prepared with 'foreign' peas.

If you are going to make this dish out of season, you can use frozen *petits pois*. The result may not be quite as good, but it is well worth being able to prepare this exquisite soup all the year round.

Preparation time: 20 minutes
Cooking time: 30 minutes
Serves: 4

$\frac{1}{2}$ *small onion, finely chopped*
50 g/2 oz pancetta or unsmoked streaky
  bacon, finely chopped
50 g/2 oz butter
500 g/1 lb peas, shelled or 225-g/8-oz
  frozen petits pois, thawed
30 ml/2 tablespoons chopped fresh parsley
5 ml/1 level teaspoon sugar
salt and freshly ground black pepper
1·5 litres/2$\frac{1}{2}$ pints home-made meat stock
  (see page 138)
300 g/11 oz arborio or other Italian rice
50 g/2 oz freshly grated Parmesan cheese

Put the onion, pancetta or bacon and half the butter in a large saucepan and fry for about 3 minutes, until the onion is pale golden. Add the peas, parsley, sugar and seasonings and cook over low heat, for 10 minutes if you are using fresh peas, or 3 to 4 minutes if you are using frozen peas. Add a few tablespoons of hot stock if the peas become too dry.

Meanwhile bring the stock to the boil and add it to the peas. Return to the boil and add the rice. Cover and cook for 15 to 20 minutes until the rice is tender, stirring occasionally. Adjust the seasonings. Remove from the heat, add the remaining butter and sprinkle with Parmesan. Mix well and serve.

Gnocchi Verdi *Spinach and ricotta gnocchi*

EMILIA-ROMAGNA

Ricotta is a favourite ingredient in this region of Italy, and these *Gnocchi*, flavoured with spinach, are quite delicious. Don't worry if they are not all the same size. Incidentally, they are also called *malfatti*, meaning badly made, but the name refers only to their shape!

Preparation time: 40 minutes
Cooking time: 15 minutes
Serves: 4

1 kg/2 lb spinach, cooked, or 500 g/1 lb
*   frozen leaf spinach, thawed*
salt and freshly ground pepper
2 eggs
200 g/7 oz ricotta cheese
200 g/7 oz flour
2·5 ml/½ teaspoon grated nutmeg
100 g/4 oz freshly grated Parmesan cheese
100 g/4 oz butter

Cook the spinach with 5 ml/1 level teaspoon salt in a covered pan for 5 minutes. Drain and, as soon as it is cool enough to handle, squeeze all the water out with your hands. Chop the spinach very finely or pass it through the coarsest setting of a food-mill. In a bowl, beat the eggs together and mix in the ricotta. Beat again. Mix in the flour, spinach, nutmeg and half the Parmesan cheese. Taste and adjust seasoning.

Dust your hands with flour and form the mixture into balls, the size of large marbles. Place them on a tray and chill in the refrigerator for about 30 minutes.

To cook the gnocchi, bring 4 litres/7 pints of salted water to the boil in a very large saucepan. Add the gnocchi, a dozen at a time. Retrieve them with a slotted spoon 3 to 4 minutes after the water returns to the boil, transfer them to a dish, dot with a little butter, sprinkle over a little cheese, and keep them warm while you continue cooking the remaining mixture.

Meanwhile melt the remaining butter in a small saucepan. Just before serving spoon the butter over the cooked gnocchi. Sprinkle with the remaining cheese and serve at once.

Gnocchi di Patate *Potato gnocchi*

PIEDMONT

Gnocchi made with potatoes are found all over northern Italy. They are dressed with different sauces: with melted cheese and butter in Piedmont; with butter, grated cheese and sage in Lombardy and Veneto; and with *Pesto* in Liguria. They are also delicious with tomato sauce.

It is difficult to state the exact amount of flour, because some potatoes absorb more flour than others.

Preparation time: 40 minutes
Cooking time: 5 minutes
Serves: 4

1 kg/2 lb floury potatoes, boiled and skinned
5 ml/1 level teaspoon salt
5 ml/1 level teaspoon baking powder
about 275 g/10 oz flour
1 egg, beaten
75 g/3 oz butter
2 garlic cloves, lightly crushed
3–4 sage leaves, torn
75 g/3 oz freshly grated Parmesan cheese

Sieve the potato on to a working surface. Sprinkle the salt and the baking powder on to the flour in a bowl and mix well, then add the beaten egg and half of the flour to the potatoes. Knead, adding more flour gradually, until the mixture is soft, smooth and slightly sticky. Shape the mixture into rolls, about 2·5 cm/1 inch in diameter, and then cut into 2 cm/¾ inch pieces.

To shape the gnocchi, take a fork and hold it with the prongs resting on the working surface at an angle of about 45 degrees. Take each piece of dough, dust it with flour, press it lightly with the thumb of your other hand against the inner curve of the prongs and, with a quick downwards movement, flip it towards the end of the prongs. The gnocchi should be concave on the thumb side, and convex with ridges on the fork side.

Put 5 litres/8 pints water into a large saucepan and bring to the boil. Do not put salt in the water, because salt tends to make the gnocchi stick together. Meanwhile, make the sauce. Put the butter, garlic and sage leaves in a small heavy saucepan and cook slowly. The sauce is ready when the butter foam has disappeared and the butter is light golden. Discard the garlic and keep the sauce warm.

Drop about 30 gnocchi at a time into the boiling water. Cook for about 20 seconds after they come to the surface, then lift them out and transfer to a heated dish. Pour over a little sauce, sprinkle with some cheese and keep warm. Repeat until all the gnocchi are cooked. Pour the remaining sauce over, sprinkle with Parmesan and serve.

Gnocchi Verdi

114

Gnocchi di Semolino *Semolina gnocchi*

LAZIO

This recipe is a variation of *Gnocchi di Semolino*, mentioned in what is reputed to be the first recipe book written in Imperial Rome, by Marcus Gavius Apicius. Apicius' name is synonymous with gluttony. Having eaten his way through a considerable fortune, he could not face the prospect of the lean days ahead and killed himself. His *Gnocchi* are fried, rather than baked, and then covered with honey, a favourite ingredient of ancient Roman cooking.

Preparation time: 40 minutes (plus 30–35 minutes cooling)
Cooking time: 10 minutes
Oven temperature: 230°C, 450°F, Gas Mark 8
Serves: 4–5

1 litre/1¾ pints milk
salt
225 g/8 oz semolina, preferably Italian
3 egg yolks
75 g/3 oz freshly grated Parmesan cheese
pinch of grated nutmeg
100 g/4 oz butter

Heat the milk with a pinch of salt in a heavy saucepan until just simmering and add the semolina in a thin slow stream, beating rapidly with a fork or a whisk. Keep the mixture at simmering point and continue beating for about 10 minutes, until the semolina has formed a thick paste and can be drawn away from the sides of the pan.

Remove from the heat and allow to cool a little, then add the egg yolks, 30 ml/2 tablespoons Parmesan, the grated nutmeg, 25 g/1 oz of the butter and salt. Mix well together.

Moisten a cold surface—marble or formica—with a little cold water, turn the semolina out on to it and spread to a thickness of 1 cm/½ inch. Allow it to cool completely.

With a 4-cm/1½-inch biscuit cutter cut the semolina into rounds. (Moisten the cutter every now and then in cold water to make the cutting easier.) Place the gnocchi in a buttered rectangular ovenproof dish large enough to fit them all in a single layer, slightly overlapping.

Melt the remaining butter in a small saucepan, and pour over the gnocchi. Sprinkle with the remaining Parmesan and bake in the oven for 5 to 10 minutes until a light golden crust has formed. Allow to settle for 5 minutes before serving.

Gnocchi alla Parigina *Choux pastry gnocchi*

VALLE D'AOSTA, PIEDMONT

I ate these delicious *Gnocchi* in the Valle d'Aosta, the northern province of Italy bordering France. I think they have been given the name *alla Parigina* (Parisian style) because they are made with choux pastry, which is typically French.

Preparation time: 45 minutes
Cooking time: 15 minutes
Oven temperature: 200°C, 400°F, Gas Mark 6
Serves: 4

225 ml/8 fl oz milk
100 g/4 oz butter
salt and freshly ground black pepper
150 g/5 oz flour, sifted
4 eggs
150 g/5 oz Gruyère cheese, grated
pinch of grated nutmeg
béchamel sauce made with 568 ml/1 pint milk, 65 g/2½ oz butter and 50 g/2 oz flour (see page 133)
freshly grated Parmesan cheese

To make the pastry, heat the milk, butter, salt and pepper in a saucepan. Bring to the boil, then remove from the heat and add the flour, all at once. Beat thoroughly until well blended. Return to the heat and cook for 2 to 3 minutes, stirring all the time. The mixture should be smooth and form a ball in the pan. Take care not to over-beat or the mixture will become fatty. Allow to cool for a few minutes, then blend in the eggs, one at a time, beating well after each addition. Add the Gruyère and nutmeg and stir well. Leave to cool, stirring from time to time.

With the pastry make balls, the size of small walnuts flouring your hands often to stop them sticking. Drop the balls, about a dozen at a time, into a large saucepan of boiling salted water. They are cooked in about 3 minutes after the water comes back to the boil, and when they come to the surface.

Lift them from the water gently with a slotted spoon and put them in a large shallow ovenproof dish, which has been warmed and buttered. Cover with béchamel sauce. Bake in the oven for about 15 minutes, until the top is golden and slightly crusty. Serve with grated Parmesan.

DESSERTS

Zuccotto *Florentine pudding*

TUSCANY

A Florentine will tell you that *Zuccotto* is shaped like the cupola of the city's cathedral. Its name in fact means *little pumpkin*. *Zuccotto* is now made commercially all over Italy, but it is quite easy to make at home.

There is great satisfaction in making the beautiful decoration: segments of cocoa powder and icing sugar coming together at the top. Or you can make it either completely white or all brown.

Preparation time: 45 minutes (plus 12 hours chilling)
Oven temperature: 200°C, 400°F, Gas Mark 6
Serves: 8–10

50 g/2 oz almonds, skinned
50 g/2 oz hazelnuts
45 ml/3 tablespoons brandy
45 ml/3 tablespoons Cointreau
45 ml/3 tablespoons Maraschino or other sweet liqueur
250 g/9 oz Madeira cake, cut into 0·5-cm/ ¼-inch thick slices
150 g/5 oz bitter chocolate
450 ml/¾ pint whipping cream
100 g/4 oz icing sugar, sifted

For the decoration:
30 ml/2 level tablespoons icing sugar
15 ml/1 level tablespoon cocoa, sifted

Put the almonds and the hazelnuts on separate baking sheets, place in the oven for 5 minutes and then, with a rough towel, rub off as much of the hazelnuts' skin as you can. Roughly chop both kinds of nuts and set aside.

Mix the three liqueurs together and moisten the cake with the liqueurs. Completely line the inside of a 1·5-litre/ 2½-pint pudding basin with the cake.

Melt 25 g/1 oz of the bitter chocolate in a small bowl over a pan of boiling water.

Meanwhile cut the remaining chocolate into small pieces. Whisk the cream with the icing sugar until stiff and into it fold the almonds, hazelnuts and the chocolate pieces.

Divide the cream mixture into two halves and spoon one half into the mould, spreading it evenly all over the cake lining the bottom and sides. Fold the melted chocolate into the other half of the cream. Spoon it into the mould to fill the cavity. Moisten the remaining cake slices with the liqueurs remaining and use to cover the pudding. Cover the mould with cling film and refrigerate for at least 12 hours.

Before serving, remove the cling film and place a piece of greaseproof paper and then a piece of cardboard over the base of the pudding. Invert the pudding on to the paper and cardboard and place on a board.

To decorate the pudding, cut out a circle of greaseproof paper 26 cm/10½ inches in diameter. Fold into eighths. Open out and cut out each alternative section without cutting through at the top. Dust the whole dome with the sifted icing sugar. Mix together the 30 ml/2 level tablespoons of icing sugar with the cocoa. Place the cut out piece of paper over the dome and sprinkle the cocoa and sugar mixture in the cut out sections. Remove the paper carefully without spoiling the pattern. Transfer the pudding to a round serving dish, using the cardboard for support. Serve chilled.

Cassata Siciliana *Sicilian gâteau*

SICILY

This is certainly the best known Sicilian pudding. You can buy it ready made and frozen all over Italy, but it is better if you can make it yourself. Although it takes a long time to prepare, it is easy to make and tastes absolutely delicious.

Preparation time: 1 hour (plus 4 hours chilling)
Serves: 8

500 g/1 lb ricotta cheese
175 g/6 oz caster sugar
150 ml/¼ pint single cream
225 g/8 oz crystallised fruit
pinch of ground cinnamon
75 g/3 oz bitter chocolate, chopped into small pieces
25 g/1 oz pistachio nuts, blanched, skinned and chopped
100 ml/4 fl oz Maraschino or an orange-flavoured liqueur
500 g/1 lb Madeira cake, cut into 1-cm/ ½-inch thick slices

For the icing:
600 g/1 lb 4 oz icing sugar, sifted
105 ml/7 tablespoons water
15 ml/1 tablespoon lemon juice

Press the ricotta through a sieve with the back of a wooden spoon into a bowl. Stir in the sugar with the cream.

Cut 100 g/4 oz of the crystallised fruit into small pieces, reserving the best fruit for decoration. Add to the ricotta mixture with the cinnamon, chocolate, pistachios and half the liqueur. Mix thoroughly.

Line an 18-cm/7-inch cake tin with greaseproof paper. Use half of the Madeira cake to line completely the base and sides. Moisten the cake in the tin with half of the remaining liqueur. Spoon in the ricotta mixture, cover with a layer of sliced cake and moisten with the remaining liqueur. Cover with cling film and chill for at least 3 hours.

Cut a piece of cardboard the size of the cake and cover with greaseproof paper. Place it over the cake in the tin and turn it over. Put the cake on a board.

Place the icing sugar, water and lemon juice in a heavy saucepan. Heat gently, stirring, until the mixture is warm but not boiling. It should be thick enough to coat the back of a spoon evenly. Pour the icing over the cake and let it run down the sides. Smooth it over with a palette knife.

Put the cake back into the refrigerator to allow the icing to set.

Just before serving place the cake on a dish and decorate with the reserved crystallised fruit. Serve chilled.

Il Meringone di Sant' Ambroeus   *Frosted meringue cake*

LOMBARDY

Very often in Milan dining at friends' houses, I have been given a beautiful looking meringue cake, lavishly decorated, made by one of the smartest pâtisseries there. It turned out to be one of the simplest puddings, easily made at home, even if you do not succeed in decorating it quite so elaborately.

Preparation time: 20 minutes (plus at least 4½ hours chilling)
Cooking time: 1 hour
Oven temperature: 150°C, 300°F, Gas Mark 2
Serves: 8

5 egg whites, at room temperature
275 g/10 oz caster sugar
450 ml/¾ pint whipping cream
25 g/1 oz pistachio nuts, blanched, skinned and roughly chopped
50 g/2 oz plain or bitter chocolate, finely chopped
25 g/1 oz candied orange peel (see page 137)
30 ml/2 level tablespoons icing sugar
chocolate chips and candied violets

Draw 23-cm/9-inch circles on two sheets of non-stick paper and place the paper on two baking sheets.

Whisk the egg whites until stiff. Fold in 50 g/2 oz of the sugar and continue whisking until the mixture is very stiff and glossy. Fold in the remaining sugar with a metal spoon. Spread the meringue mixture over the two paper circles, gently smoothing the tops with a palette knife.

Place the meringues in the oven and bake for 20 minutes. Reverse their shelf positions and bake for a further 20 minutes. Reduce the heat to 140°C, 275°F, Gas Mark 1 and bake for a further 20 minutes. The meringue should be slightly brown on the top and just firm to the touch. Allow to cool and then carefully remove from the paper.

Meanwhile whisk the cream until soft peaks are formed. Fold in the pistachios, chocolate pieces, candied peel and icing sugar. Spread three-quarters of the cream mixture between the meringue rounds and the remaining cream on the top.

Cover and put the meringue cake into the freezer for at least 4 hours. Half an hour before serving remove from the freezer and place in the refrigerator.

To serve, decorate with chocolate chips and candied violets.

Macedonia di Frutta   *Fresh fruit salad*

PUGLIA

Macedonia is a region of northern Greece and southern Yugoslavia whose population comprises a number of different races. Thus the name *macedonia* indicates the variety of fruit in this dish. It is a favourite of Italians, who love to end their meals with fruit.

Preparation time: 20 minutes (plus at least 6 hours chilling)
Serves: 8

2 apples, peeled, cored and cut into 1-cm/ ½-inch cubes
2 pears, peeled, cored and cut into 1-cm/½-inch cubes
2 bananas, sliced
750 g/1½ lb assorted fruit, such as peaches, apricots, cherries, grapes, plums, figs, nectarines, stoned or seeded and cut into small pieces
50 g/2 oz sugar, or more according to taste
juice of 4 oranges
juice of ½ lemon

Place the fruit in a glass bowl. Sprinkle with sugar and pour over the fruit juice. Mix well and refrigerate for at least 6 hours.

Bonissima *Walnut and honey pie*

EMILIA-ROMAGNA

The Italian name of this pudding means 'very good'. It is somehow reminiscent of Bakewell tart and treacle tart, mixed together. In Emilia-Romagna *Bonissima* is served without cream—as applies to a lot of Italian puddings—but I think in this instance cream improves it.

Preparation time: 30 minutes (plus 2½ hours chilling)
Cooking time: 35–40 minutes
Oven temperature: 190°C, 375°F, Gas Mark 5
Serves: 6–8

150 g/5 oz plain flour
pinch of salt
75 g/3 oz caster sugar
grated rind of 1 lemon
75 g/3 oz butter, cut into small pieces
1 egg, beaten

For the filling:
150 g/5 oz walnuts
150 ml/¼ pint honey
50 ml/2 fl oz rum

For the icing:
100 g/4 oz icing sugar
15 ml/1 tablespoon water
2·5 ml/½ teaspoon lemon juice

Place the flour, salt, sugar, lemon rind and butter in a bowl. Rub the mixture together until it looks like fine breadcrumbs. Stir in the egg and knead the mixture quickly into a ball. Wrap the pastry in cling film and leave in the refrigerator to chill for 1 hour.

Blanch the walnuts in boiling water for 15 seconds. Strain, and as soon as they are cool enough to handle, remove as much of the skin as you can. Roughly chop the walnuts and add to the honey and rum. Mix well together.

Roll out two-thirds of the pastry and use to line the base and sides of a 18-cm/7-inch flan dish or loose-bottomed tin. Fill with the walnut and honey mixture. Roll out the remaining pastry and use to cover the pie. Seal the edges and leave in the refrigerator for 30 minutes.

Bake the pie in the oven for 35 to 40 minutes until golden brown. Leave to cool.

Sift the icing sugar and place in a small saucepan with the water. Heat gently, stirring until the mixture is warm, but not hot. It should coat the back of a spoon and be smooth and glossy. Add the lemon juice, stir well and spoon over the top of the pie. Allow to set.

Cut the pie into wedges before serving.

Torrone Molle *Chocolate nougat dessert*

LOMBARDY

Commercially-made *Torrone* is a long white bar, chewy and full of nuts. This home-made version, however, is quite different, being dark in colour and soft. It is quick and easy to prepare and one of the tastiest puddings you could eat.

Preparation time: 20 minutes (plus 4 hours chilling)
Serves: 8–10

225 g/8 oz unsalted butter, softened
225 g/8 oz granulated sugar
100 g/4 oz cocoa
1 egg, plus 1 egg yolk
100 g/4 oz almonds, blanched and coarsely chopped
100 g/4 oz plain biscuits, crumbled
30–45 ml/2–3 tablespoons brandy, orange-flavoured liqueur or rum

Cream together the butter and sugar in a bowl until light and fluffy. Gradually add the cocoa and beat thoroughly until it is completely absorbed. (Although it takes a while and might seem a large quantity of cocoa, it *will* work into a stiff but well-blended mixture.)

Lightly beat together the egg and the yolk and add slowly to the butter cream, stirring until they are well blended. Add the remaining ingredients, mix well, and spoon the mixture into a 500-g/1-lb loaf tin, lined with greaseproof paper.

Refrigerate for 4 hours or overnight and turn out on to a serving dish.

Decorate with rosettes of cream and crystallised violets.

Zabaione *Marsala custard*

PIEDMONT

Although *zabaione* is usually eaten immediately it is cooked, it is also delicious frozen and served as an ice. Before freezing add 200 ml/7 fl oz of double cream which has been whipped with 30 ml/2 tablespoons of iced water and 30 ml/2 tablespoons of icing sugar.

Preparation and cooking time: 15 minutes
Serves: 6

4 egg yolks
65 g/2½ oz caster sugar
100 ml/4 fl oz Marsala

Put the egg yolks and sugar in the top half of a double saucepan or in a bowl, beat them together and add the Marsala and mix. Place the saucepan or bowl over a saucepan of simmering water and heat gently, whisking the mixture until it is very thick and creamy and forms soft peaks.

Pour into 6 tall glasses. Serve immediately with boudoir biscuits.

Tiramesu *Coffee trifle*

VENETO

The Venetians call this a 'pick me up'; doubtless because of the coffee and brandy the trifle contains. In Italy the cake would be layered with a soft variety of cream cheese called *mascarpone*, but this is difficult to find in this country. I find that egg custard is a very good substitute.

Preparation time: 40 minutes (plus 6 hours minimum for chilling)
Serves: 8

500 g/1 lb Madeira cake, sliced and cut into 0.5-cm/¼-inch squares
225 ml/8 fl oz freshly-made strong black coffee
10 ml/2 teaspoons coffee essence
150 ml/¼ pint brandy

For the custard:
4 egg yolks, size 1
100 g/4 oz caster sugar
45 ml/3 level tablespoons cornflour
568 ml/1 pint milk
2.5 ml/½ teaspoon vanilla essence

For the decoration:
60 ml/4 level tablespoons grated plain or bitter chocolate
whipped cream

First make the custard. Whisk the egg yolks and sugar together in a bowl until light and fluffy. Add the flour, spoon by spoon, beating it constantly with a wooden spoon, until it is thoroughly absorbed. Warm the milk in a saucepan and then slowly pour on to the egg yolk mixture, stirring constantly. Strain the mixture into the top of a double saucepan or into a heavy-based saucepan. Stir over a very gentle heat, using a wooden spoon, until the sauce thickens sufficiently to coat the back of the spoon and an occasional bubble breaks the surface. Cook for a further 2 minutes. Remove the pan from the heat and stir in the vanilla essence. Set aside for later use.

Completely cover the bottom of a 22.5-cm/9-inch round glass bowl with pieces of Madeira cake. This should use up about one-quarter of the cake. Mix together the coffee, coffee essence and the brandy in a small bowl and brush about one-quarter of the liquid over the cake in the bowl to produce a marbled effect. Spoon one-third of the custard over the layer of cake and smooth it over. Repeat this operation until all the ingredients are used up, finishing with a layer of cake lightly soaked with liquid.

Chill the trifle in the refrigerator for at least 6 hours. Just before serving, sprinkle the grated chocolate over the top of the trifle and decorate with piped whipped cream.

Lattaiolo Marchigiano *Milk pudding from Urbino*

MARCHE

This pudding is reminiscent of baked custard. It is homely and simple with no pretences. In central Italy, where it is very popular, it is served cold, cut into cubes and covered lavishly with icing sugar, but I think it is even better with cream poured over it at the table.

Preparation time: 10 minutes
Cooking time: 1 hour
Oven temperature: 180°C, 350°F,
*   Gas Mark 4*
Serves: 4–6

2 eggs
50 g/2 oz sugar
50 g/2 oz plain flour
250 ml/9 fl oz milk
250 ml/9 fl oz single cream
2·5 ml/½ level teaspoon ground cinnamon
pinch of grated nutmeg
grated rind of ½ lemon
pinch of salt
icing sugar

Beat the eggs thoroughly with the sugar until pale. Add the flour, beating all the time, and then, very slowly, fold in the milk and cream. Add the cinnamon, nutmeg, lemon rind and salt. Pour the mixture into a 900-ml/1½-pint buttered pie dish.

Bake for about 1 hour, until a skewer inserted in the middle comes out clean. Leave to cool for at least 1 hour.

When cold, turn out on to a dish. Cut into 5-cm/2-inch cubes and sprinkle lavishly with icing sugar.

Torta alle Mandorle e all'Arancia *Almond and orange tart*

VENETO

Tarts such as this one are rarely served in Italy. Perhaps it is a legacy of Venice's trading links with the Middle East—oranges and almonds being favourite ingredients there.

Preparation time: 15 minutes (plus 1½ hours
*   chilling)*
Cooking time: 40–45 minutes
Oven temperature: 180°C, 350°F,
*   Gas Mark 4*
Serves: 6–8

225 g/8 oz plain flour
pinch of salt
90 g/3¼ oz caster sugar
100 g/4 oz unsalted butter, cut into small
*   pieces*
1 egg yolk
15 ml/1 tablespoon brandy
225 g/8 oz granulated sugar
225 g/8 oz ground almonds
juice of 3 medium oranges
rind of 1 orange
25 g/1 oz candied orange and lemon peel
*   (see page 137)*

Sift the flour and salt together on to a working surface, preferably a marble slab, or a bowl. Make a well in the centre, add the caster sugar, butter, the egg yolk and brandy and work these four ingredients together with your fingertips until well blended. Gradually work in all the flour and then gather the mixture into a ball. Knead lightly until smooth. Wrap the pastry in cling film or foil and leave to chill in the refrigerator for at least 1 hour.

To make the filling mix together all the remaining ingredients.

Allow the dough to soften a little and then roll out two-thirds of it. Use this to line a 21·5-cm/8¼-inch loose-bottomed fluted flan tin. Fill with the almond and orange mixture. Roll out the remaining pastry and use to cover the tart. Press the edges together to seal and refrigerate for 30 minutes.

Bake the tart in the oven for 40 to 45 minutes until the pastry has shrunk a little and is golden brown. Remove from the oven and leave to cool.

Serve cold, with or without cream.

Torta di Noci   *Walnut cake*

CAMPANIA

This is the best walnut cake I have ever eaten. The recipe comes from Naples, near Sorrento, where the best Italian walnuts come from. Although it is usually served without cream, I sometimes accompany it with cream or with coffee ice-cream. It is delicious whatever you do, but be careful to buy fresh walnuts, as the rancidity of stale walnuts can ruin a dish.

Preparation time: 20 minutes
Cooking time: 50 minutes
Oven temperature: 180°C, 350°F,
*   Gas Mark 4*
Serves: 8

6 eggs, separated
250 g/9 oz sugar
3 drops of vanilla essence
50 g/2 oz plain flour
250 g/9 oz walnuts, finely chopped
icing sugar

Grease a 23-cm/9-inch loose-bottomed or spring-form release cake tin and line its base.

Beat the egg yolks with the sugar until pale and creamy. Add the vanilla essence and the flour and mix thoroughly. Add the walnuts gradually, mixing well after each addition. Whisk the egg whites until stiff and fold into the egg and sugar mixture.

Spoon the walnut mixture into the prepared tin. Bake in the oven for about 50 minutes, until risen and firm to the touch. Remove from the tin and allow to cool.

Sprinkle with sifted icing sugar to serve.

Budino alla Valdostana   *Caramel-custard pudding*

VALLE D'AOSTA, PIEDMONT

This is a very simple pudding from the Alpine region on the border with France.

Preparation time: 20 minutes (plus
*   10 minutes cooling)*
Cooking time: 45 minutes
Oven temperature: 190°C, 375°F,
*   Gas Mark 5*
Serves: 6

568 ml/1 pint milk
rind of ½ lemon
115 g/4½ oz granulated sugar
50 g/2 oz butter
50 g/2 oz flour
3 eggs, separated

In a saucepan, bring the milk with the lemon rind and 65 g/2½ oz of the sugar to the boil. Remove from the heat and keep warm.

Put the rest of the sugar and 30 ml/2 tablespoons of water into a flameproof 2-litre/3½-pint charlotte mould or a 20·5-cm/8-inch cake tin (not non-stick). Dissolve the sugar over moderate heat, without stirring, and boil for 10 to 15 minutes until a light-brown colour. Remove from the heat and tip the mould to coat the inside evenly with the caramel.

Retrieve the rind from the warm milk and discard.

Melt the butter in a saucepan over low heat and add the flour. Cook for 1 minute, stirring constantly. Remove from the heat and add 200 ml/7 fl oz of the milk. Return the saucepan to the heat and mix until the milk has been absorbed. Slowly add the remaining milk, stirring constantly. Bring to the boil and, still stirring, simmer for 2 minutes. Allow to cool for about 10 minutes, then add the egg yolks, one at a time, mixing well after each addition.

Whisk the egg whites until stiff and fold them into the milk mixture. Then pour the mixture into the caramel-lined mould. Place in a roasting tin half filled with water and bake in the oven for about 45 minutes, until set. Remove from the oven and allow to cool for 10 minutes.

To unmould the pudding, warm the mould over low heat for 30 seconds, then place a dish over the mould, turn upside down and give it a few sharp jerks. Refrigerate until needed.

Granita di Caffe *Coffee ice*

Granita is a water ice served in a glass, broken into innumerable ice crystals. You can have a fruit or a coffee *Granita* when you sit out of doors at the cafe on a hot afternoon. I think the coffee *Granita* is by far the best, especially if you put a table-spoon of whipped cream, slightly sugar-ed, on the top.

*Preparation time: 10 minutes (plus
   3–4 hours freezing)*
Serves: 6

*30 ml/2 level tablespoons sugar or more
   according to taste*
*600 ml/1 pint freshly-made strong black
   coffee*

Put the sugar into the hot coffee and stir until dissolved. Taste and add more sugar if necessary. Pour the coffee into 2 freezing trays and leave to cool. When the coffee is cold, put the trays in the freezer for 30 minutes, then remove and break up the coffee ice. Return the trays to the freezer. Repeat the operation of breaking the coffee ice about every 30 minutes until granular.

Serve in individual glass bowls.

Bomba Gelata and Granita di Caffe

Bomba Gelata *Iced bombe*

SICILY

A delicately-coloured cream and lemon mould studded with candied fruit, this dessert sums up everything that one con-nects with Sicilian desserts. The iced custard should line the whole mould, but the custard can be thawed slightly if the first attempt to line the mould is unsuc-cessful.

*Preparation time: 45 minutes (plus 9–10
   hours chilling)*
Serves: 6–8

5 eggs, separated
150 g/5 oz caster sugar
568 ml/1 pint milk
grated rind of 1 lemon
150 ml/¼ pint whipping cream
*25 g/1 oz almonds, blanched and finely
   chopped*
25 g/1 oz candied fruit, finely chopped
15 ml/1 level tablespoon icing sugar

Put the egg yolks and the caster sugar in a bowl and beat for about 5 minutes, until pale and fluffy. Then place the bowl over a saucepan of gently simmering water.

Pour the milk into another saucepan and heat gently. When the milk is very hot, but not boiling, pour it slowly over the yolks and sugar, beating all the time. Cook for about 15 minutes, until the custard has thickened and will coat the back of a wooden spoon. Do not allow the custard to boil or it will curdle. Remove the bowl from the heat and add the grated lemon rind. Put the bowl in a basin of cold water and allow to cool, stirring frequently.

When the custard is cold, pour it into a shallow plastic container, cover with a lid or foil and freeze for about 6 hours. Beat the custard every 30 minutes during the freezing.

Place a 1·2-litre/2-pint bombe mould or pudding basin in the freezer.

When the custard is frozen, spoon it into the chilled mould, lining the bottom and sides of the mould with it and push into the sides with a spoon, leaving a hole in the middle. Return the mould to the freezer.

Whisk the cream and then fold in the almonds, candied fruit and icing sugar. Spoon the whipped cream mixture into the centre of the mould and return to the freezer. Freeze for at least 4 hours.

Half an hour before serving, cover the mould with a dish, turn over and put the dish with the mould on it in the refrigerator. By the time you wish to serve the bombe you should be able to lift the mould off the pudding. If the pudding is still frozen, dip the mould quickly into very hot water, and then lift off.

Le Bisse *S-shaped biscuits*

VENETO

A *bissa* is a water snake in Venetian dialect, which explains the name of these little S-shaped biscuits. They are to be found in any bakery or pâtisserie in Venice, but they can easily be made at home.

Preparation time: 15 minutes (plus 1 hour chilling)
Cooking time: 15–20 minutes
Oven temperature: 220°C, 425°F, Gas Mark 7
Makes about 35 biscuits

3 eggs
175 g/6 oz caster sugar
150 ml/¼ pint vegetable oil
grated rind of 1 lemon
550 g/1 lb 2 oz plain flour
pinch of salt

In a large bowl, whisk the eggs with the sugar until pale and creamy. Add the oil and lemon rind, then fold in the flour and salt. Knead well. Wrap the dough in cling film and chill it in the refrigerator for about 1 hour.

Grease two large baking sheets.

Take little balls of dough and roll them out into sausage shapes a little more than 1 cm/½ inch thick and 12·5 cm/5 inches long. Shape each one into the form of an S and arrange on the baking sheets. Bake in the oven for 5 minutes. Reduce the heat to 180°C, 350°F, Gas Mark 4 and bake for a further 10 to 15 minutes until pale golden.

Torta di Mele alla Piemontese

Torta di Mele alla Piemontese *Apple and breadcrumb cake*

PIEDMONT

This is an unpretentious cake which is quite delicious. Traditionally the *Torta* is served without cream.

Preparation time: 30 minutes
Cooking time: 45 minutes
Oven temperature: 170°C, 325°F, Gas Mark 3
Serves: 8

150 g/5 oz butter
1·25 ml/¼ teaspoon ground cinnamon
1·5 kg/3 lb dessert apples, peeled, cored and thinly sliced
150 g/5 oz fresh dried breadcrumbs
115 g/4½ oz sugar
60 ml/4 level tablespoons apricot jam
juice of ½ lemon

In a heavy saucepan put 15 g/½ oz of the butter, the cinnamon and the sliced apples and cook, covered, over low heat for 20 to 25 minutes until the apples are soft.

Meanwhile melt the remaining butter in a small non-stick saucepan and, a little at a time, add the breadcrumbs and sugar. Stir constantly, until golden.

Gently heat the jam and lemon juice in a saucepan until melted. Set aside.

Spread one-third of the breadcrumbs mixture on the bottom of a buttered 21·5 × 11-cm/8 × 4-inch loaf tin, cover with half the warm jam mixture and then half the cooked apples. Repeat these layers, ending with the breadcrumbs mixture.

Bake in the oven for about 45 minutes. Allow to cool in the tin and then turn the pudding out on to an oval dish.

Cassata di Sulmona
Cassata made with butter cream

ABRUZZI-MOLISE

When one talks of *Cassata* abroad people immediately think of *Cassata Siciliana*. This *Cassata* from Abruzzi is less well-known but equally delicious. It is made with butter cream instead of ricotta.

Preparation time: 45 minutes (plus 3 hours chilling)
Serves: 6–8

For the praline:
30 ml/2 level tablespoons sugar
7·5 ml/1½ teaspoons water
5 ml/1 teaspoon lemon juice
25 g/1 oz almonds, blanched and skinned

For the cassata:
75 g/3 oz sugar
100 g/4 oz unsalted butter, softened at room temperature
3 egg yolks
25 g/1 oz hazelnuts, skinned, toasted and chopped
25 g/1 oz cooking chocolate, broken into small pieces
15 g/½ oz cocoa, sifted
350 g/12 oz Madeira cake, cut into 0·5-cm/¼-inch thick slices
75 ml/3 fl oz rum

For decoration:
150 ml/¼ pint double cream, whipped
grated chocolate
almonds or hazelnuts

To make the praline, lightly brush a cold surface with oil. Heat the sugar, water and lemon juice in a small heavy saucepan over very low heat. When the sugar has dissolved, boil rapidly until the syrup is golden. Remove from the heat and add the almonds. Mix thoroughly, pour quickly on to the oiled surface before the mixture sets and leave to cool. Then put the praline between two sheets of greaseproof paper or into a polythene bag and crush finely with a rolling pin.

To make the cassata, place the sugar and butter in a bowl and beat together until pale. Add the egg yolks, one at a time, beating well after each addition. Divide the mixture into three parts: to the first add the praline, to the second the hazelnuts and the chocolate, and to the third the sifted cocoa.

Line a 900-g/2-lb loaf tin with foil, and butter the foil. Line the tin with a layer of the cake slices, brush with some of the rum and spread over the praline cream. Cover with a second layer of cake, brush with a little more rum and spread over the hazelnut and chocolate cream. Cover with a third layer of cake, brush with rum and spread over the cocoa cream. Cover with the last layer of cake and brush with the remaining rum. Cover with foil and leave in the refrigerator to chill well.

To serve, turn the cassata on to a serving dish. Decorate with whipped cream, grated chocolate and nuts.

Pere alla Crema del Lago di Como
Stewed pears with lemon and liqueur-flavoured cream

LOMBARDY

This recipe comes from Tremezzo, a resort which used to be favoured by the English. Indeed the similarity of the recipe to syllabub makes one wonder whether it was introduced to the town by an English cook.

Preparation time: 20 minutes (plus 1 hour chilling)
Cooking time: 10–20 minutes
Serves: 6

3 pears, Williams if available
grated rind and juice of ½ lemon
165 g/5½ oz caster sugar
75 ml/3 fl oz Grappa (eau de vie) or brandy
300 ml/½ pint whipping cream

Peel the pears, cut them in half and remove the cores. To prevent discolouration immediately put them into a bowl of water to which a few drops of lemon juice have been added. Dissolve 100 g/4 oz of the sugar in 225 g/8 fl oz water over gentle heat. When the sugar has dissolved, put in the pears and cook for 10 to 20 minutes until tender.

Meanwhile make the cream mixture. Add the remaining sugar to the lemon rind and juice and the liqueur and stir until dissolved. Whip the cream until stiff and slowly fold the liqueur mixture into it.

When the pears are cooked, lift them out of the syrup. (The syrup can be used to flavour a fruit salad.) Place them in individual bowls, cover with the cream and chill for 1 hour before serving.

SAUCES

Ragù *Bolognese sauce*

EMILIA-ROMAGNA

In Italy every cook or restaurant claims to prepare the best *Ragù*, which can only mean that the variations are endless. Some cooks add chicken livers, others mushrooms, some use minced beef and minced pork or sausage, some add cream at the end, others milk at the beginning and so on. One thing always applies: you should cook the *Ragù* over a very low heat and for a long time. This is a good standard recipe, on which you can base your own variations if you wish.

Preparation time: 20 minutes
Cooking time: 2–2½ hours
Makes: enough to dress 4 servings of pasta

25 g/1 oz butter
45 ml/3 tablespoons vegetable oil
2 slices of unsmoked streaky bacon, finely
    chopped
1 small onion, finely chopped
1 small carrot, finely chopped
1 small celery stick, finely chopped
1 small garlic clove, finely chopped
1 bay leaf
25 ml/1½ tablespoons tomato purée
225 g/8 oz best minced beef
100 ml/4 fl oz dry white wine
100 ml/4 fl oz meat stock (see page 138)
salt and freshly ground black pepper

Heat the butter and oil in a saucepan and cook the bacon for 1 minute. Add the onion and, when it begins to soften, the carrot, celery, garlic and bay leaf. Stir and cook for 2 minutes. Add the tomato purée and cook over a low heat for 30 seconds. Put in the minced beef and cook briskly for 3 to 4 minutes until the meat has lost its raw colour. Add the wine and boil for about 4 minutes until the liquid has almost evaporated. Discard the bay leaf and pour in the stock. Mix well, season and simmer, uncovered, for about 2 hours, adding a little warm water if the sauce becomes too dry.

For a more delicate sauce, add 30 ml/2 tablespoons of cream before serving.

Maionese *Mayonnaise sauce*

Contrary to what many people think, mayonnaise is not difficult to make. Home-made mayonnaise is so much better than the commercial kind that it is well worth practising a few times and mastering the art of it. It is important that all the ingredients should be at room temperature. Mayonnaise made with vegetable oil is lighter and more delicate than that made with olive oil. Italians always use lemon juice, never vinegar.

Preparation time: 15–20 minutes
Makes: 225–300 ml/8–10 fl oz

2 egg yolks
salt
225–300 ml/8–10 fl oz mixture of olive
    and vegetable oil such as sunflower or
    corn
30 ml/6 teaspoons lemon juice
freshly ground black pepper (optional)

Place the egg yolks in a bowl and beat together with a wooden spoon or with an electric beater set at medium speed. Add a little salt and beat again until pale. Add the oil, drop by drop, beating all the time. Continue adding the oil drop by drop while beating, until the sauce is the consistency of double cream. Then, still beating, add 5 ml/1 teaspoon of the lemon juice. This will thin the sauce a little. Add more oil, in a thin stream, stopping every now and then to allow the yolks to absorb the oil while you beat. When the sauce has thickened again add another 5 ml/1 teaspoon lemon juice. Continue to add the oil and lemon juice in stages until all the oil and lemon juice have been used. Taste and adjust the seasonings.

If you want a thinner mayonnaise, add a little less oil.

Should the mayonnaise curdle, break another egg yolk into a clean bowl, beat well and then add the curdled mayonnaise, one teaspoonful at a time.

Pesto *Basil sauce*

LIGURIA

This sauce for dressing pasta has a mysterious and very particular taste given to it by the mixture of basil, pine nuts and olive oil. It is the most famous of Ligurian sauces and the Genoese, who created it, say that good *Pesto* can only be made with the basil which grows near Genoa, since it needs hot sun and Mediterranean breezes. Although there may be something in this, I think that *Pesto* is still very good when made with basil grown in Britain. Unfortunately it is rarely obtainable, but you can grow your own in a sunny sheltered spot in the garden or on a sunny window sill.

The sauce freezes very well, so you can make it in quantity while basil is in season. When you prepare the sauce for freezing, omit the garlic, the cheese and the cream. Add them after the sauce is thawed, just before serving.

When you make a rich vegetable soup or a *Minestrone*, add a tablespoon of *Pesto* before serving, mix properly, and your soup will remind you of your Mediterranean holiday.

Makes: enough to dress 4 servings of pasta

50 g/2 oz basil leaves
2 garlic cloves
30 ml/2 level tablespoons pine nuts
pinch of rock salt
freshly ground black pepper
40 g/1½ oz freshly grated Parmesan cheese
30 ml/2 tablespoons freshly grated Romano
  cheese (Parmesan can be substituted for
  the Romano cheese)
100 ml/4 fl oz olive oil
30 ml/2 tablespoons double cream

Pesto made in the mortar
Preparation time: 20 minutes

Put the basil, whole garlic cloves, pine nuts and rock salt in a mortar and grind until the mixture is a paste. Add the grated cheeses and blend thoroughly in the oil a little at a time, while stirring with a wooden spoon. When all the oil has been added, adjust the seasonings and fold in the cream.

Pesto made in the blender or in the food processor
Preparation time: 5 minutes

Combine the basil, whole garlic cloves, pine nuts, salt, pepper and olive oil in a blender and mix at high speed. Blend until very creamy. Transfer mixture to a bowl and fold in the grated cheeses and cream. Mix thoroughly.

Pesto

131

Sugo di Pomodoro al Naturale   *Plain tomato sauce*

This is a recipe for a tomato sauce prepared without any fat. It can be used on its own or as a base for sauces which involve other ingredients. You can also use it to dress a dish of spaghetti—in which case you should add 50 g/2 oz of butter or 25 g/1 oz of butter and 30 ml/ 2 tablespoons of olive oil before you heat it.

If you are using the sauce at once, reheat it gently and serve. Otherwise it will keep for 4 to 5 days in the refrigerator in a covered container, or you can freeze it.

Preparation time: 5 minutes
Cooking time: 30 minutes
Makes: enough to dress 4 servings of pasta

500 g/1 lb tomatoes, skinned and quartered,
   or 396-g/14-oz can tomatoes, with their
   juice
1 small onion, quartered
1 celery stick, chopped
1 garlic clove, chopped
1 bay leaf
1 sprig of parsley
5 ml/1 level teaspoon sugar
salt and freshly ground black pepper

Put all the ingredients into a small saucepan, bring to the boil, then simmer, uncovered, for 30 minutes until the sauce has thickened. Stir occasionally to prevent sticking and, if the sauce gets too dry, add a little warm water during cooking.

Discard the bay leaf and either rub the sauce through a sieve with the back of a wooden spoon or purée in an electric blender or through a food mill until smooth.

Sugo di Pomodoro alla Napoletana   *Neapolitan tomato sauce*

CAMPANIA

This sauce should be prepared with San Marzan tomatoes, a kind of very sweet tomato grown near Naples. In the last year or two I have seen fresh plum tomatoes here in Britain. They are imported from France and are excellent. Use them for this sauce if you can find them, otherwise use best canned plum tomatoes.

Preparation time: 10 minutes
Cooking time: 10 minutes
Makes: enough to dress 6 servings of pasta

1 kg/2 lb fresh tomatoes, skinned, or
   a 793-g/28-oz can plum tomatoes, with
   their juice
1 garlic clove, crushed
100 ml/4 fl oz olive oil
5 ml/1 level teaspoon sugar
5–6 basil leaves, torn, or 15 ml/1 tablespoon
   chopped fresh parsley, or 7·5 ml/½ table-
   spoon oregano
salt and freshly ground black pepper

Combine all the ingredients in a small saucepan and simmer gently, over moderately low heat for about 10 minutes, until the oil has separated from the tomatoes.

Salsa Besciamella *Béchamel sauce*

Béchamel was already a popular sauce in Italy when the French claimed it as their own in the seventeenth century. It is called *Besciamella* or *Balsamella* and is flavoured with nutmeg.

Preparation and cooking time: 10 minutes
Makes: 225 ml/8 fl oz sauce

300 ml/½ pint milk
50 g/2 oz butter
40 g/1½ oz flour
pinch of grated nutmeg
salt and freshly ground black pepper

Pour the milk into a saucepan and bring to simmering point. In another, heavy, saucepan, melt the butter over low heat, then blend in the flour. Cook, stirring constantly, for 30 seconds. Remove the pan from the heat and, with a wooden spoon, beat the hot milk into the flour and butter mixture, a little at a time, until all the milk has been absorbed and the sauce is completely smooth.

Add the seasonings and return the saucepan to the heat. Slowly bring the sauce back to the boil and simmer, still stirring, for 2 to 3 minutes for a medium coating sauce or for 5 to 6 minutes for a thicker sauce.

Salsa Rossa Agrodolce per il Bollito
Sweet-and-sour tomato sauce for boiled meat

A piquant sauce to accompany a plate of succulent sliced meat.

Preparation time: 5 minutes
Cooking time: 35 minutes
Makes: enough to dress 4–5 servings of meat

15 ml/1 level tablespoon onion, very finely
    chopped
1 garlic clove, finely chopped
15 ml/1 tablespoon chopped fresh parsley
4–5 basil leaves (optional)
25 g/1 oz butter
30 ml/2 tablespoons olive oil
500 g/1 lb fresh tomatoes, skinned and
    roughly chopped, or 396-g/14-oz can
    plum tomatoes, drained
15 ml/1 tablespoon wine vinegar
15 ml/1 level tablespoon sugar
pinch of ground cinnamon
salt and freshly ground black pepper

In a saucepan fry the onion, garlic, parsley and basil leaves (if used) gently in the butter and oil for about 5 minutes, until the onion is soft. Add the tomatoes and cook, stirring frequently, until the tomatoes separate from the oil, about 10 minutes. Purée the sauce in a liquidiser or food processor.

Return it to the saucepan and add the vinegar, sugar and cinnamon. Taste and add the seasonings. Bring to the boil, then simmer for 20 minutes, adding a few tablespoons of warm water if the sauce becomes too dry.

Salsa Verde *Italian green sauce*

A piquant green sauce served with boiled meats or boiled or steamed fish.

Preparation time: 15 minutes
Makes: enough to dress 4 servings

30 ml/2 tablespoons finely chopped parsley
30 ml/2 level tablespoons capers, chopped
1 garlic clove, finely chopped
4 anchovy fillets, mashed
2·5 ml/½ level teaspoon Dijon mustard
5 ml/1 teaspoon red wine vinegar (for meat)
    or 15 ml/1 tablespoon lemon juice (for
    fish)
100 ml/4 fl oz olive oil

Put the parsley, capers, garlic, anchovy fillets and the mustard in a bowl and mix thoroughly. Add the vinegar or lemon juice and stir. Slowly add the olive oil, beating all the time.

The sauce can be stored, covered, in the refrigerator for 2 to 3 weeks.

Salsa di Noci *Walnut sauce*

LIGURIA

The walnuts lend a very subtle flavour to this delicious Ligurian sauce. Do be sure to use fresh walnuts. Serve the sauce with spaghetti or tagliatelle.

Preparation time: 10 minutes
Cooking time: 10 minutes
Oven temperature: 150°C, 300°F,
Gas Mark 2
Makes enough to dress 4 servings of
pasta

25 g/1 oz white bread, crustless
100 g/4 oz walnuts, preferably blanched
and skinned
1 garlic clove
30 ml/2 tablespoons freshly grated
Parmesan cheese
45 ml/3 tablespoons olive oil
45 ml/3 tablespoons double cream
25 g/1 oz butter

Soak the bread in warm water for 10 minutes. Drain and squeeze out the water. In a blender or food processor combine the walnuts, bread and garlic and blend until creamy. Transfer this mixture to a large ovenproof bowl and add the Parmesan cheese, oil, cream and butter. Place the bowl in the oven for 10 minutes. Dress cooked spaghetti or tagliatelle with the sauce and serve at once.

Sugo di Pomodoro Crudo *Uncooked tomato sauce*

CAMPANIA

This sauce, which is always served with spaghetti, is extremely easy to make, but needs very fresh and first quality ingredients. You can build up your own variations of this sauce, substituting seasonings or adding different ingredients to this basic mixture.

Preparation time: 15 minutes (plus 6 hours
marinating)
Makes: enough to dress 4 servings of
spaghetti

350 g/12 oz ripe tomatoes, skinned and
seeded
75 ml/5 tablespoons olive oil
1 garlic clove, finely sliced
10–12 basil leaves, each torn into 2–3
pieces, or 30 ml/2 tablespoons chopped
fresh parsley
salt and freshly ground black pepper

Cut the tomatoes into thin wedges. Place them in a bowl with all the other ingredients, mix well and leave to marinate for at least 6 hours. Dress cooked spaghetti with the sauce and serve at once.

Ingredients

Fortunately, it is now possible to buy nearly all of the ingredients of good Italian food in this country. I have tried here to describe those which are less familiar and suggest substitutes for foods which are not so easy to obtain.

Meats

Pancetta is similar to bacon, but, instead of being smoked, it is cured in salt and spices. It is rolled like a large salami and can be bought in a single thick piece or cut into paper-thin slices, whatever is required. When lean and of very good quality it can be eaten raw, and its taste resembles that of a strong-flavoured *prosciutto*. In Italy it is sometimes served in a dish of *affettato*, which literally means 'sliced' and consists of different cold pork cuts, such as ham, salami and *mortadella*. *Pancetta* is often used in Italian cooking to add moisture and flavour to the meat or vegetable with which it is cooked. It is now obtainable in many British delicatessens, but if you cannot find it a good substitute is unsmoked streaky bacon.

Mortadella is the prize sausage of Bologna, indeed in northern Italy it is often referred to as *bologna*. It is made from different cuts of pork, encased together in a large roll, and then boiled or steamed. The authentic *mortadella* is very large, measuring up to 40 cm/16 inches in diameter and is flavoured with pistachio nuts, coriander and wine.

Prosciutto is world famous and needs little introduction. The *prosciutto* from Parma is reputed to be the best, though, personally, I find that one produced in San Daniele in Venezia Giulia is at least as delicious and sometimes even better. Unfortunately you cannot buy it here, but look out for it when you are next in Italy. Like *prosciutto di Parma*, it should be pale red in colour, sweet and tender, and it should be thinly cut, but not so much so—as it seems to me to be fashionable nowadays—that you can hardly taste it. In Italy *prosciutto* is eaten with melon, the scented deep yellow kind, or with fresh figs, or in a dish of *affettato*. The *prosciutto di montagna*, which is made in quite a few Italian regions, is stronger, of a coarser texture and redder in colour.

Luganega is a sausage made from the shoulder of the pig and should contain Parmesan cheese. Like *pancetta*, it is also often used to add flavour and fat to a dish, and can be grilled or fried, then cooked in stock and wine or in tomato sauce. If you cannot find *luganega*, substitute any mild coarse-grained Continental pork sausage.

Scaloppine or **piccate** are cut, like escalopes, from veal fillet, but across the grain instead of with it. As escalopes are easier to obtain in this country, substitute these but cut them into small rectangles first, allowing three or four per person.

Cheeses

Parmesan is the best of the finely-grained hard cheeses known as *grana*, and made only in Emilia. Authentic *Parmesan* has the name *Parmigiano-Reggiano* printed all over its rind. There are other *grana* types made, and in greater quantities than *Parmesan*, principally south of Milan in the Po valley, where the latter are collectively known as *grana padano*.

Parmesan should be pale buff-yellow in colour, slightly moist, and have a crumbly texture. It is essential for most pasta dishes and for many other recipes too. When first class, it is quite exquisite eaten by itself with a glass of red wine.

Unfortunately good *Parmesan* is a rarity in Britain; so when you do see some, buy a large piece. It keeps for weeks in the refrigerator. Cut the piece into small wedges, weighing about 200 g/ 7 oz each, and wrap each one in a double thickness of foil. If, after some time, the cheese becomes too dry, wrap it in a damp piece of cloth for 24 hours to restore some of the moisture. Afterwards, remove it from the cloth, rewrap it in the foil and return it to the refrigerator.

Do not grate more *Parmesan* than you need, because it will lose its flavour. And do not discard the crust. Use it in soups, such as minestrone, and with pasta and beans or tripe.

Never buy ready-grated cheese sold in packets or cartons. If you are unable to find good *Parmesan* in a piece, an alternative, though not a substitute, is a mature Cheddar cheese.

Mozzarella. Genuine *mozzarella* is made from buffalo's milk, but to meet the demand for this cheese, cow's milk is also used. If Italian *mozzarella* is unobtainable, substitute *Bel Paese* (see below).

A *mozzarella* usually weighs about 200 g/7 oz. For many recipes you will not need this much. Keep the rest in a bowl in the refrigerator covered with salted water for up to 3 days.

I am much indebted to Marcella Hazan for suggesting, in her book *The Second Classic Italian Cookbook*, how to improve the *mozzarella* available outside Italy. Here is her method: grate the cheese on the large holes of a grater or in the food processor, using the shredding disc. Put it into a bowl, add 45 ml/3 tablespoons of olive oil and leave for at least 1 hour before using.

Bel Paese is a well-known and common cheese now in Britain. *Bel Paese* cooks quite well and can replace *mozzarella* in a recipe, although the taste will not be the same. *Bel Paese* should be semi-soft and creamy looking.

Pecorino is made from sheep's milk, throughout central and southern Italy. There you can buy it as a soft, fresh cheese or hard and matured. In Britain, only the hard *pecorino*, called Romano, is available; use it for cooking in the same way as *Parmesan*.

Ricotta is a soft, white, bland milk product. It is used a great deal in Italian cooking, especially in Emilia-Romagna for pasta fillings, and in southern Italy for desserts, cheesecakes and tarts. It is obtainable in many delicatessens, but a good substitute can also be made at home, with little trouble and cost. *Ricotta* is highly perishable and should be consumed within 24 hours.

Preparation time: 5 minutes
Cooking time: 15 minutes
Makes: about 225 g/8 oz
1 litre/1¾ pints milk
20 ml/4 teaspoons lemon juice
5 ml/1 level teaspoon salt

Bring the milk to the boil in a saucepan, reduce the heat and add the lemon juice and salt. Mix well and simmer for 15 minutes, stirring frequently.

Line a sieve with a double thickness of muslin and strain the liquid through into a mould or bowl. Leave the cheese to drip for 1 hour, stirring it twice during this time.

Provolone. Originally made from buffalo's milk, like *mozzarella*, *provolone* is now made from cow's milk or from a combination of the two. It looks like a large *mortadella* sausage and has a bland taste and a rubbery texture. As the fresh *provolone* from southern Italy is not available in this country, it is advisable to buy *provola*, a smaller version of *provolone*. *Provola* is shaped like a very large egg, and then tied on strings to dry it.

Fontina. One of the best Italian cheeses; sadly it is unusual to find the genuine article in this country, and nothing equals the *fontina* you get in Val d'Aosta. *Fontina* is a good melting cheese, tasting not unlike a mild *Gruyère*. It is the main ingredient of the famous Piedmontese *fonduta*, similar to the Swiss fondue.

Gorgonzola. A blue-veined cheese from Lombardy which has become the Italian equivalent of the British Stilton. Originally allowed to mould naturally, this process is now accelerated by the use of copper wire. It is also used in conjunction with Italian cream cheese to make *Dolcelatte*, a milder, creamier version of the real thing.

Rice

Italian rice is shorter and rounder than long-grain rice. It takes longer to cook, and the grains, while keeping a firm 'soul'—as the Italians say (meaning inner firmness)—adhere to each other in a soft creamy consistency. This is a vital factor in the making of risotto.

The most commonly exported Italian rice is *arborio*, which is sold loose in Italian shops or in packets under different brand names. Although it is impossible to make a real risotto with long-grain rice, it is the best substitute if Italian rice is unobtainable.

Funghi

Dried mushrooms are wild *boletus edulis*, the kind called *cèpes* in France and *porcini* in Italy. They have a highly concentrated flavour due to the drying process and they are ideal for seasoning sauces, risottos or meat, or they can be added to cultivated fresh mushrooms if you want a stronger flavour. They are reconstituted by soaking in warm water for about 20 minutes. The water should not be discarded, but can be strained and added to the sauce during the cooking.

Dried mushrooms are expensive, but as they are very concentrated you need only use a very small quantity. They are sold in 10-g/⅓-oz packets and are available not only in Continental delicatessens, but also in many other good food stores.

Herbs

In Italy the use of herbs is regional, in the sense that particular herbs are connected with different dishes, which, in their turn, always suggest a region. While they are an important element in homely Italian cooking, herbs are always used with caution, with one or two notable exceptions.

One of these is *pesto*, made from basil, the most typically Italian of all herbs. It should always be used fresh, because its taste changes when dried. It is an annual which is quite easy to grow indoors on a sunny window sill. The scent of oregano immediately brings to mind the food of the south, while marjoram, a very similar herb, is used a lot on the Riviera. Rosemary is the favourite herb of Tuscany and all of central Italy (it is used to flavour roasted and grilled meat). Sage is the herb of the north, probably because it goes so well with butter, the cooking fat of northern Italy. And then, of course, there is parsley. The Italian variety differs from English parsley in looks—its leaves are flat and open instead of being tightly curled—although the taste is very similar. You can use either.

Dried herbs are not as good as fresh and they can become too pungent or musty. Always smell them first and use them with care.

Garlic

An ancient plant native to the Mediterranean, garlic was originally used primarily for its medicinal properties: purifying the blood, clearing the skin and aiding the digestion. It is a fallacy to assume that all Italian cooking is highly flavoured with garlic—this theory has gained credibility only because the majority of Italian emigrants to Britain and the United States have come from the south, where more garlic is used than anywhere else.

Often it is used whole, lightly browned and discarded before continuing the cooking. But the most important thing to remember is never to let garlic burn or else it becomes bitter and can ruin any dish.

When you buy garlic, look for large full heads. When the clove is dry, use less garlic, because the taste is sharper and stronger.

Olive oil

Olive oil is the basic cooking fat in Liguria, where some of the best oil comes from, and in central and southern Italy. Good olive oil should be heavy, greenish in colour and taste like green olives. If you can find *Extra vergine* olive oil, which is top quality and comes from the first pressing of the olives, buy a large quantity. Decant it into glass bottles and seal it firmly or else it can become rancid.

In some cases vegetable oil can be substituted for olive oil, in which case I have noted this in the list of ingredients. These include dishes in which the taste of olive oil would be obtrusive, and also when the oil is to be used for frying. But in many sauces and other cooked dishes as well as in any salad, olive oil is an essential because of its unique flavour.

Dried breadcrumbs

Home-made breadcrumbs give the best results, so avoid using the commercially-prepared types. To make: put day-old bread, white or brown, into a blender or processor and work till you have fine crumbs. Spread these over a baking tray and bake in a preheated oven, 150–170°C, 300–325°F, Gas Mark 2–3, for 15–20 minutes or until crisp and pale golden. Cool, then store in an airtight jar.

Salad dressing

The salad ingredients, after being washed, should be well dried. It is important to add the dressing at the last minute before you serve salad, which will otherwise go soggy. The classic Italian dressing consists of olive oil, wine vinegar and salt.

It is difficult to state how much oil, vinegar or salt you should add, as so much depends on the fruitiness of the oil or the sharpness of the vinegar, and of course on personal taste. However, as a rough guide, a green salad for four would probably need 45 ml/3 tablespoons of oil, 7·5 ml/½ tablespoon of vinegar and 2·5 ml/½ teaspoon of salt. The oil should coat each leaf and the vinegar should be just recognisable, but should not kill all other tastes.

Pepper is not considered an essential ingredient, nor is garlic, but I like to smear the cut side of a garlic clove around the salad bowl. Do taste your salad before bringing it to the table.

The Italians say that you need four people to dress the salad: a generous person to pour the oil, a mean one to add the vinegar, someone wise to sprinkle the salt and, lastly, a patient soul to toss it. Certainly you should toss it many, many times. Some say 36 times is the secret of a successful salad!

Candied orange peel

In Sicily, where citrus fruits are abundant, orange and citron peel are both candied at home. I always buy citron peel, but candied orange peel (*scorzette di arancia candite*) is very easy to make. The taste is infinitely superior to the mixed peel you can buy, and it is much more economical.

Preparation time: 30 minutes, plus 48 hours soaking and 12 hours drying
Cooking time: 20 minutes
Makes: about 350 g/12 oz

6 thin-skinned oranges, such as blood oranges, washed and quartered
About 225 g/8 oz sugar

Carefully remove the flesh from the orange quarters, using a small, sharp knife. Put the peel in a bowl, cover with cold water and leave to soak for 48 hours, changing the water at least four times.

Drain the peel, lay it on a dry cloth, and dry for 20 minutes; then cut it into very thin strips.

Weigh the peel and set aside. In a separate bowl, put the same weight of sugar. Place the sugar in a heavy-bottomed saucepan over very low heat. When the sugar has dissolved, raise the heat and boil until a rich golden colour. Add the orange peel and an extra 30 ml/2 tablespoons of sugar and cook, stirring constantly, for about 8 minutes until the sugar is dissolved again.

Brush several large baking sheets with vegetable oil and spread the peel over them, separating the strips with a fork. Allow to dry for 12 hours or longer. Store in a screw-top jar.

Stock

Italian stock (*brodo*) is lighter than French stock. It is essential to nearly all clear soups in which pasta, rice or vegetables are cooked, and to most risottos. It is very economical to make and keeps up to four days in the refrigerator, or it can be frozen. When freezing stock, I always put handy quantities, convenient for use in risottos, in separate containers.

Preparation time: 10 minutes
Cooking time: 3–4 hours
Makes: about 1·75 litres/3 pints

1 carrot
1 onion
1 celery stick
1 tomato
*500 g/1 lb assorted bones (chicken, veal and beef, not
  lamb or pork)*
500 g/1 lb scraps of the same types of meat
5 ml/1 level teaspoon salt
4–5 peppercorns

Put the whole vegetables and the rest of the ingredients into a large pan, cover with 2 litres/ 3½ pints of cold water and bring slowly to the boil.

Remove the scum which rises to the surface in the first few minutes of cooking. Cover and simmer gently for 3 to 4 hours.

Strain the stock into a bowl, allow to cool and then refrigerate, uncovered. When cold, remove the fat from the surface. If you are not using the stock immediately, cover, then freeze or refrigerate it. If refrigerated and not used within 4 days, bring it back to the boil, simmer for 10 minutes, allow to cool and return it to the refrigerator—but always use up within a week of making.

Pasta

The best pasta is imported from Italy, under brand names such as De Cecco, Braibanti, Brambilla, Agnesi, and Buitoni. The English-made pasta,

Making stuffed tortellini

Record, or the pasta made for some of the multiple stores by Pasta Foods, in wholemeal varieties as well, is also good, although limited in the shapes available. Fresh pasta, as opposed to the dried kind, can be found too, and may be flavoured in various ways, spinach being the most common (see recipe, right, and page 140).

When you buy pasta, make sure that it states on the packet that it is made from 100 per cent durum wheat or *semola di grano duro.*

There are many different pasta shapes—over five hundred in Italy, according to somebody who once had the patience to count them, of which about fifty are common. Their names differ depending on where you are, which makes the whole thing quite muddling. With each recipe I have indicated the shape or shapes of pasta best suited for a particular sauce. If you want to use another shape, remember that long pasta is ideal with tomato, cream or fish sauces, while short tubular pasta have cavities and hollows in which to retain meaty, heavier sauces.

Home-made pasta

In Emilia-Romagna pasta (*pasta all'uovo*) is made with just flour and eggs, unlike other regions of Italy, where milk, olive oil or water are sometimes added. Home-made flat pasta, such as *tagliatelle*, *fettuccine* or *tagliolini*, is usually served with meat sauces or vegetable sauces, but it is delicious with any dressing. Try serving *tagliatelle* dressed with butter, double cream and *Parmesan* cheese, for example. Home-made pasta can also be used to make all the varieties of stuffed pasta, the most common being *canelloni* and *ravioli.*

It is impossible to say precisely how long it takes to prepare, particularly if the dough is to be rolled out by hand. But however long, the result is worth it. If the pasta is rolled out by machine the process is much quicker, especially if you use an electric machine, which does everything for you.

Use plain white flour and size 2 eggs. The amount of flour depends upon the size and the absorbing-capacity of the eggs, so that it is not possible to give a hard-and-fast quantity. Usually the proportion is about 90–100 g/3½–4 oz of flour per egg. It is, however, more difficult to work with a large amount of flour. As your skill and speed develop, try to work with more flour and as tough a dough as you can. The firmer the dough, the better the pasta.

A long thin rolling pin (4 cm/1½ inches thick, 80 cm/32 inches long) is essential, as is a large, smooth working surface.

Makes: enough for 3–4 servings

165–200 g/5½–7 oz flour
2 eggs, size 2
pinch of salt

1. Place the flour in a mound on a clean working surface. Make a well in the centre and break the eggs into it. Add the salt. Start beating the eggs with a fork, gradually incorporating the flour from the inside of the well. When the paste thickens, mix in the rest of the flour with your hands and quickly work it until the mixture forms a mass. If it is too sticky and moist, add a bit more flour, but do not overdo it.
2. Set the mixture aside and clean the surface, using a knife to scrape off the crumbs. Wash your hands, removing all dough, then dry them.
3. Lightly flour the working surface and your hands, and start kneading the dough with the heel of your hands. Continue kneading for about 10 minutes, until the dough is elastic. Wrap the dough in cling film and let it rest for at least 20 minutes and up to 3 hours.
4. Lightly flour the working surface and the rolling pin. Pat the dough into a flattish shape and start gently rolling away from you. After each roll rotate the dough so that it remains circular. Repeat until the dough is about 20 cm/8 inches in diameter.

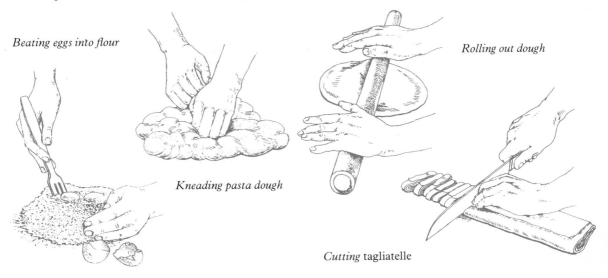

Beating eggs into flour

Kneading pasta dough

Rolling out dough

Cutting tagliatelle

5. Now proceed to the final rolling process. This is slightly tricky, but once you have done it several times it will seem simple.

Dust the working surface and the rolling pin lightly with flour. Curl the far end of the pasta around the middle of the rolling pin and roll it upwards towards you. As you do this, quickly slide your hands towards the ends of the pin, gently stretching the pasta away from the centre while you roll the pin backwards and forwards very rapidly. Continue with these movements, applying 'pull', not weight, with your hands, until you have rolled up nearly the whole circle of pasta. While it is still wrapped around the rolling pin, lift and turn it about 45°, making sure that the sheet is even, smooth, and has no holes or creases. If the dough is a little sticky, dust the surface again with flour. Repeat this rolling and stretching process until the sheet becomes nearly paper thin (about 1 mm/$\frac{1}{32}$ inch) and about 35 cm/14 inches in diameter, but try not to take longer than 10 minutes or the pasta will become dry and lose elasticity. This thin sheet is called *sfoglia*.

6. If you are making stuffed pasta (*ravioli*, *cappelletti* or *canelloni*), the *sfoglia* must not be allowed to dry. Proceed immediately with the recipe. If you are making cut pasta (*tagliatelle*, *lasagne*, etc.), place a clean dry towel on the table and lay the *sfoglia* on it, letting one-third of the sheet hang over the edge of the table. The pasta is ready to cut when it is dry to the touch and begins to look leathery—about 30 minutes, depending on the temperature of the room.

Tagliatelle. Bring the *sfoglia* to a working surface. The easiest way to carry it is to roll it on to the rolling pin. Fold the *sfoglia* over into a flat roll, approximately 8 cm/3 inches wide. With a sharp broad-bladed knife, cut the *sfoglia* into 1-cm/$\frac{1}{2}$-inch wide strips. Try to cut the noodles all the same width. When all the pasta has been cut, unfold the *tagliatelle* and leave them to dry for a minimum of 10 minutes.

You can cook them straight away—they will take only a few seconds—or you can let them dry and then store them, just like bought pasta.

If you want to store *tagliatelle*, take a few strands and curl them round your hands, as you would with wool. Place these little nests on a clean tea towel and allow to dry completely. This dried pasta takes a little longer to cook than freshly-made pasta.

Fettuccine. Proceed as for *tagliatelle*, but cut into 0·5-cm/$\frac{1}{4}$-inch wide strips.

Lasagne. Bring the *sfoglia* to the working surface. Cut it into 10 × 15 cm/4 × 6 inch rectangles. If you are using a hand-cranked machine, the width of the dough is already determined by the machine.

For cutting the *sfoglia* into shapes, see the individual recipes.

Spinach pasta (*pasta verde*) is usually used for *lasagne* or *tagliatelle*. Cooking time for spinach pasta is slightly longer than for ordinary pasta.

225 g/8 oz spinach or 150 g/5 oz frozen leaf spinach,
  thawed
pinch of salt
250 g/9 oz plain flour
2 eggs, size 2

Cook the spinach with a little salt in a covered saucepan for 10 minutes if using fresh spinach or 5 minutes if using frozen. Stir occasionally to prevent it from sticking. Drain and cool. Squeeze out as much water as you can with your hands. Chop very finely.

Make the green pasta according to the basic instructions for home-made pasta on page 139, adding the spinach with the eggs. It is impossible to give the exact quantity of flour. Work the flour into the egg and spinach mixture gradually until the mixture has incorporated as much flour as possible without becoming too dry and brittle.

Roll out the *sfoglia* (see left) and shape as required.

Cooking pasta

For cooking home-made pasta, *except tagliatelle*, which takes 30 seconds from the time the water returns to the boil, follow the directions given in the individual recipes.

For bought pasta, boil at least 4 litres/7 pints of water in a very large saucepan for 500 g/1 lb pasta. And add 45 ml/3 tablespoons of salt for each 500 g/1 lb of pasta.

When the water is boiling very rapidly, drop in all the pasta at once. Turn up the heat and quickly return the water to the boil. The cooking time varies from about 8 minutes, according to the size and thickness of the pasta. Watch it carefully and check it soon after the water returns to the boil. Cook until it is *al dente*, just firm to the bite.

Agnesi, one of the leading Italian pasta manufacturers, has pioneered a new method of cooking bought pasta—it cooks for most of the time in water that has gone off the boil. The advantages are: even if you leave it in the hot water for a minute or two too long, the pasta does not become gluey. Therefore there is no need to stand over the saucepan.

Put the pasta into a large saucepan of rapidly boiling salted water and stir well. Cover the pan and bring the water back to the boil quickly. Then immediately uncover the pan, stir well and boil for 2 minutes. Turn off the heat and stir again. Cover the pan with a folded tea towel and replace the lid. Leave the pasta to stand in the pan for the length of time given in the manufacturer's instructions for normal cooking. Then drain the pasta quickly and serve.

Wine

The Italians were making wine as long ago as the 9th century BC in what, even in ancient times, was called Enotria or 'Land of Wine'. Blessed with a very favourable climate, Italy is today the largest wine-producing country in the world, with some 3·5 million acres of vines scattered throughout the peninsula and in Sicily, Sardinia and the smaller islands. At 93 litres per head per annum, she also has the second biggest consumption—and about a quarter of the population is said to be concerned with viticulture, vinification and the wine trade.

Yet it is only since the early 1970s that Italian wines have become so popular with the British public—both the inexpensive *vini da tavola* and the more costly but still moderately priced quality wines. The proliferation of Italian restaurants, holidays abroad and the efforts of the Italian Institute for Foreign Trade have all contributed to this remarkable success story but most important of all was the introduction, in 1963, of the system of Denominazioni di Origine, the best known of which is Denominazione di Origine Controllata, equivalent to the French Appellation d'Origine Contrôlée. For, by strictly defining the various wine areas and by specifying and controlling all aspects of wine cultivation and production, these regulations have greatly improved standards of quality and thereby increased significantly the confidence of the consumer. To date there are more than 200 districts that have achieved D.O.C. classification.

Red, white and rosé, sweet and dry, still and sparkling, Italy offers a splendid variety of interesting and pleasurable wines for every occasion. It would be impossible to list them all but the estimated total is in excess of three thousand—from Albana to Zagarolo! Here is a baker's dozen of the better known ones by region, with short descriptions and recommendations for drinking.

Piedmont

Barolo—one of the finest Italian red wines: deep-coloured with a powerful bouquet and a pronounced, rich flavour. Goes well with red meat and game.

Barbera—the best is supposed to be from around Asti: ruby-red, ageing to garnet, with a pleasant vinous bouquet and medium body. A good all-purpose red wine.

Asti spumante—one of the world's most popular and best-known sparkling wines: light and refreshing with a delicious, sweet, honeyed taste of muscat. Always serve well chilled, either as an aperitif or with dessert.

Veneto

Soave—a deservedly famous white wine: straw-yellow in colour with a delicate, fruity nose and a dry flavour reminiscent of almonds. An excellent accompaniment to hors d'oeuvre, fish and white meats.

Valpolicella—from a district north of Verona: ruby-red, elegant and fruity. Goes well with pasta, veal and poultry.

Bardolino—an attractive, fresh red wine similar to Valpolicella. Most experts prefer it!

Emilia-Romagna

Lambrusco—the effervescent red wine from the province of Modena that has been so successful in America: dry or slightly sweet, with a lively, distinctive character. Particularly complementary to rich dishes like the local *zampone*, stuffed pig's trotter.

Tuscany

Chianti—possibly the most renowned wine of Italy. *Classico* comes from the best part. *Riserva* means more than three years old. Ruby, maturing to red; dry, well-structured style becoming softer with age. Considerable variations depending on situation and producer. For drinking with poultry, meat and game.

Brunello di Montalcino—reputedly the greatest of Italian red wines: big and warm and of marked personality. A wine that will keep and improve for many years.

Umbria

Orvieto—*secco* (dry) or *amabile* (semi-sweet) white wines characterised by their full golden colour and aromatic bouquet and flavour. Suitable with fish and poultry.

Rubesco torgiano—a relative newcomer to the international scene: red wine of notable style with a fragrant bouquet and a subtle, balanced flavour. Also worth looking for is **Torre di Giano**, Rubesco's white partner. A delightful and unusual pair to enjoy through the menu.

Marche

Verdicchio—a white wine vinified principally from the verdicchio grape: of light straw colour with a crisp, very dry taste. Just the wine to stimulate the appetite and to drink with fish of all kinds.

Lazio

Frascati—famed, since the days of the Caesars, as the wine of Rome: dry but with a generous, supple character which makes it a happy match for most food.

Sicily

Marsala—a favourite of Nelson's fleet and the most English of all Italian wines: wine fortified with brandy, varying from dry to sweet and sometimes blended with eggs, almonds and other flavours. A dessert wine, an effective pick-me-up at any time of day and an important ingredient of several delectable recipes—*scaloppine al Marsala* and *zabaione* being two worthy examples.

For buffets and barbecues, when quantity rather than quality is the order of the day, there is ample choice of sound, branded red, white and rosé table wines, usually sold in conveniently screwcapped, jumbo-size bottles. As well as Asti spumante, Italy also produces, by the Champagne and closed tank methods, some good value and extremely palatable dry sparkling wines which are well worth trying if the opportunity occurs and just right to get a party going.

Whites, still and sparkling, and rosés should always be served chilled and reds at room temperature except for some of the lighter ones such as Bardolino which are sometimes cooled, especially in summer. It is also customary to chill Lambrusco. Decanting is unusual in Italy but even so it would be wise to decant any bottle with a noticeable deposit. In any case, it is recommended to draw the corks of the finer red wines a couple of hours before they are poured. All wines should, of course, be stored horizontally in the dark, away from movement and in cool conditions at an even temperature.

In the hope that this brief introduction to Italian wines will encourage readers to take advantage of the varied and rewarding range currently available, all that is left to say, in true Italian fashion, is 'Salute!' and 'Buon appetito!'

James Long
Wine buyer for Peter Dominic

The Publishers would like to thank Pietro Negroni Limited for supplying the excellent meats and cheeses. The author and Publishers would like to acknowledge the valuable contribution made by Vera Collingwood for the loan of some of the Italian articles used in photography. The author would also like to thank Myriam de Castiglione and Thesa Ingram for their help in testing some of the recipes.

Index